Haste Ye Back

DOROTHY K. HAYNES

Haste Ye Back

 JARROLDS, LONDON

JARROLDS PUBLISHERS (LONDON) LTD
3 Fitzroy Square, London W1

AN IMPRINT OF THE HUTCHINSON GROUP

London Melbourne Sydney Auckland
Wellington Johannesburg Cape Town
and agencies throughout the world

First published 1973

This book has been set in Baskerville type, printed in Great Britain
on antique wove paper by Anchor Press, and
bound by Wm. Brendon, both of Tiptree, Essex

ISBN 0 09 113330 0

For the late C. A. E. Wolfe, M.B.E.
Warden of Aberlour Orphanage 1928–1958

The author acknowledges with thanks the use of material from the following sources: *Good Housekeeping*; *Scots Magazine*; B.B.C.; *Scottish Home and Country*; *Saltire Review*; *People's Journal* for the photograph of Dean Wolfe; and B.B.C. for photographs from *This is Your Life*.

Contents

Illustrations

Prologue

'If Candlemas Day be dry and fair,
The half o' the winter's to come and mair.
If Candlemas Day be wet and foul,
The half o' the winter's gane at Yule.'

CANDLEMAS, February 2nd, is our wedding anniversary.
This year we celebrated our silver wedding. Naturally, we
felt that something had to be done about it; but what?
Neither of us was keen on the conventional dinner, with
speeches and sentiment piled on like the confetti of twenty-
five years ago. Eventually my husband came up with the
suggestion that we should have a week at Aberlour.

Right away it seemed the only possible thing to do. We
had met there when we were children at Aberlour Orphanage. True, we had visited the place since, but now we had
a special reason for going back. The orphanage, which in
our time had held five hundred children, had been empty
for more than a year, and the inmates were being dispersed
round the country in smaller, cottage-type homes. At any
moment, we had heard, the buildings were due to come
down, and if we wanted to see our old home for the last time
we would have to act quickly.

We would have liked to take the boys with us, to show
them the place they had so often heard about, but with one
at university and one taking O-levels it just wasn't possible.
Anyway, we felt that we would be better on our own. These
nostalgic journeys can be boring for people who are not
completely in the know.

So we set off on a frosty morning at the end of January, going by car to Glasgow, and getting the train to Aviemore. Glasgow was dark, in the last January (thank goodness) of British Standard Time, and cold fog caught at the throat; but just beyond Perth the sun burst through in sudden peep-holes, like warmed patches on a frosty window, and then the train ran out of the mist and left it rolling and writhing over the fields.

The hills around Pitlochry were sifted with snow, as if an inexpert cook had sugared her cakes to hide their imperfections. Further north, the snow-line crept nearer, till at last we were travelling through a silver desert so brilliant that we had to lower the blinds against the sun. Sitting in the warm train, drinking hot coffee with a delicious sense of guilt (what right had we to go junketing like this in January?) we watched the Highland wildlife caught unawares against the whiteness. A pheasant whirred upwards, a jack rabbit leaped up in a scattering of snow, and a beautiful deer started at the noise of the train and careered away in fear.

The Cairngorms were hidden in cloud, and there were lamentations about a lack of snow on the ski slopes, but all the way down Speyside, through Grantown to Aberlour, the trees and fields were white, with just enough snow to highlight the branches. It was cold, very cold and still, with a curiously dim sun breaking through now and then, and the bus went warily down the iced roads, down through the pines and distilleries.

Aberlour is ringed with distilleries. This is whisky country, the Glenlivet area, echoing with names potent enough to drive a drinking man mad. It is cattle country, too. Where else would you see notices proclaiming the Ballindalloch Herd, the Kinermony Herd, and so on? We were drawing nearer and nearer, and the familiar names excited us like music.

Sitting at tea in the Lour Hotel we literally fidgeted at

the thought of the orphanage. Maybe . . . and yet we didn't
dare to ask if it was still standing. We had to find out for
ourselves. As soon as we'd finished our meal we slipped up
the back road, past the new bungalows and the old cot-
tages, in the cold glowing light of evening.

We could hardly believe it. There it was, like a dream,
those awful poignant dreams of wish-fulfilment, the clock
tower, the weathercock, the gables and turrets glinting
through a screen of trees. We paused, and then almost ran
towards it. Perhaps it was going to be spared, after all?

And then we noticed that the demolition had already
started. Some of the school was down. The clock in the
tower had stopped, and the box with the bell-ropes had
been removed, which was just as well, because we wouldn't
have been able to resist setting off the old hellish jangle.
We pottered about, trying to locate the old classrooms, and
then we went down to the East Wing.

It was a ruin. Blocks of stone, beams of wood, were stacked
carefully where the flower-beds had been, and window-
frames were laid in rows on the lawn. Each had its price, no
doubt; demolition and salvage were going shrewdly hand
in hand, but to us it savoured more of vandalism. The
little brook was still rippling through the churchyard,
though the rustic bridges were down. Now it was dark, with
just enough shine from the sky to see. 'I wonder . . . ?' We
tried the church door, and it opened to a smell of candle
grease and floor polish. We did not like to grope in the
belfry for the switches, so we found our way by the flame
of a cigarette lighter. Had the tiles on the floor been as
worn as that in our day?

At the back of the church we found what we had been
looking for: the new plaque, inscribed: 'To the Glory of
God, and in loving memory of the Rev. CLARENCE ALBERT
EDWARD WOLFE, B.A., M.B.E. . . .' It was difficult to read
in the tiny flame, but we felt at ease. Now we had seen it,
we could come back in the morning.

PART I

'Just like a big boarding school'

I

The new quean *

'COME and listen to me for a minute,' said my Aunt Rose, gathering my brother and me into her arms. 'How would you like to go to a big place like a boarding school? There's lots of other boys and girls there, and they've got Scouts and Guides, and you can go for picnics, and long walks in the country. . . .'

'It would be nice,' we agreed, very docile and obliging. We were twins, ten years old, and our mother had just died after a long illness. It had never occurred to us that our father might feel unable to cope any longer, nor did we know that our minister had advised him that we would be better under a woman's care. We felt that he was doing fine, and we didn't in the least mind the rather amateurish way in which he looked after us; but now that our aunt had broached the matter, a boarding school did hold possibilities. Reared on the *Magnet* and the *Schoolgirls' Own*, we felt that we would be going up in the world.

Our aunt looked relieved, if somewhat surprised at the way we accepted the situation. Probably she had been dreading the task of breaking it to us. She continued her enthusiastic build-up for some time, and when we asked where this paradise was she said : 'Abbey-lure. Away up in the Highlands.'

It was not until our father came home from work that we realised she meant Aberlour, and then our enthusiasm waned a little. We had heard of Aberlour Orphanage, and had filled, or intended to fill, collection boxes for it during

* North-east vernacular for 'girl'.

Lent, but we had never bargained for actually living there. We did not like the idea of an orphanage, we did not consider ourselves orphans. Orphans were raggedy children with running noses. However, we were assured that lots of children who went there had one or more parents living, and that there was no disgrace in being admitted for a year or two, until things sorted themselves out. 'And it *is* just like a big boarding school,' insisted our aunt, who had never been near the place.

She never did learn to pronounce the name properly. Her London tongue just couldn't get round it. Nor, in deference to our feelings, did she ever refer to it as an orphanage. Long after we had stopped caring, and wrote our address, 'The Orphanage, Aberlour, Banffshire', with great panache, she was still calling it 'The Abbey-lure', and boasting about her niece and nephew 'at school in the Scottish Highlands'.

It seems odd to me now that we left home so willingly. Probably we looked on it all as a great adventure, and did not realise till it was too late that we would be terribly homesick. The excitement lasted all through the journey northwards, and through our first breathtaking glimpse of the orphanage. We were literally dazzled by the gardens, great banks of blazing flowers, brilliant colours splashed everywhere. We were delighted at our reception by the Warden, who strode towards us smiling, gathered us in, and asked sensibly, 'Now, when did you last have something to eat?' The novelty sustained us till the moment we were separated, my brother taken to his dayroom in the West Block, and I escorted to the East Block to meet the Rectory girls.

It was overwhelming, to say the least; about thirty girls all pushing and yelling, hanging on to the Warden, and staring at me. So long as he was there, it was all right; but after he had gone, the yelling and staring continued, and I had to cope on my own. Questions were screamed at me, information was hurled at me, and I was dragged here and there, tired and shy and bewildered. Even the matron who came to my rescue terrified me. She could out-yell the lot of them.

I would have given anything, then, to call the whole thing off; and yet I would not admit, till months later, that I was homesick. I wrote home and said I liked the orphanage, I told my brother I liked it, and he said the same to me, though one had only to look at him to see that he was almost heartbroken. Leonard was a small, delicate-looking boy, later nicknamed Dainty Dinah, and to begin with I had very few chances of speaking to him. Being twins, I think we felt our separation more keenly; and then one day I saw him passing the window on his way home from the weekday church service. His hair had had the regulation crop, his feet were bare, and whereas the other boys sped along on sturdy tanned legs, he limped and trembled over the stones, wincing at the roughness. A single word of any kind would have made him weep; and here was I, heartsick and homesick too, as orphan-like as he was, my feet also bare and tender, and a pinafore over my frock. I could understand how David Copperfield felt in the blacking factory.

In the years that I was there I never once stopped wanting to get away. Everybody else shared these feelings, but they admitted them. For two years I didn't. The most I would allow myself was a share in the nostalgic sessions of 'What I'll do when I get home'.

I was rather handicapped here. Everybody, it seemed, had homes far grander than mine. Their parents, if they were to be believed, were all landed gentry, or business tycoons, or famous film stars. *My* father worked in a hosiery factory, and I hardly dared to confess that I had lived in a room and kitchen.

The plans I made for my return home were not very romantic. All I wanted was to *be* there. There was an orphanage in Lanark that used to be held over children's

heads as a threat—'If you don't behave I'll send you to
Smyllum'—just as Aberlour Orphanage was held out as
a threat to the locals. I always felt sorry for the Smyllum
orphans, uniformly dressed, walking obediently four
abreast, with two nuns following in bunchy blue skirts
and white hats. Now I envied them. They were in Lanark,
and they could see the familiar steeples in the distance, hear
the cattle in the market and the trains in the station. If I
had been there, I thought, I could have refreshed myself
every time I went out with the sight of the people I knew,
and it might even be possible to run home some day and
cling to the furniture and fight and yell and defy them to
take me back. . . .

It wouldn't have worked, of course. It was a Roman
Catholic orphanage, and we were Episcopal, and, anyway,
it was too near home; but at that time I would have changed
places with any child at Smyllum, just to be able to see my
own family now and again.

I never told my father this, and as letters were censored,
there would have been no point in trying. Nor did we complain when he came to visit us in summer, or at the spring
and New Year holidays. How could we? He was so obviously delighted with the place, and with the way we looked,
and we were so happy to be with him, and there were so
many places to go, so much to show him, that somehow
we never got round to it. It wasn't till we were twelve that
we suddenly demanded to be taken away, and by that time
I suspect that we were protesting for the sake of protesting.
We had settled down so well that we didn't have to pretend any more.

We never considered the effect the sudden demand to
be taken home would have on our father. We were enjoying ourselves too much. It was a project to be planned and
savoured for as long as possible, and we got great fun out
of meeting secretly for discussions. We composed a poem
called *The Plea*, pouring in every extravagance we could

think of, and Leonard, now promoted to a sort of junior office boy, with an extra penny a week by way of wages, was able to smuggle it down to the village and post it with the legitimate orphanage mail. We sent it in an unsealed envelope, to save money, and I've a feeling that he may have pinched the ha'penny stamp.

My father opened the envelope eagerly, expecting one of our cheerful, newsy letters. I can imagine his face as he saw what was inside.

'With weary sighs, and eyes all dimmed with tears,
We look far forward into other years,
And see ourselves in joy in Lanark town,
Far from the orphanage's fret and frown.
In Aberlour, with tears and sorrow great,
We look upon the orphanage with hate.
Like prison bars its windows seem to be,
Though near they stand to flower and grass and tree.
Oh what a difference 'tis to Broomgate Street!
To walk along there is a special treat. . . .'

We knocked the orphanage for everything. The plain, wholesome food that we polished off to the last crumb came off very badly. What we craved for, we explained, was the somewhat makeshift diet that our father provided when he came home from work.

'Oh for a Lipton's tasty cherry cake,
Or veal and ham pie, or an ashet steak!
Oh for some Lipton's ju-jubes, half a pound
For threepence, cheap as dirt upon the ground!'

It was terrible poetry, but at least it hammered out the message.

From what I have been told, my father read *The Plea* right through, turned white, and took it to the woman next door. 'Do you think it's true?' he asked, with tears in his eyes. 'They always looked so happy. . . .'

She read the manuscript with rather more detachment than my father. 'Och, get away, Ted,' she said. 'They're only having you on!'

'Do you think so?'

'Of course. I know what they'd get if they were mine!'

I don't know how many people read *The Plea*, but no doubt it was passed round, while advice was asked and given. The advice seemed to be pretty unanimous, and it appeared to tie in with my father's own ideas. At any rate, he wasn't long in coming to a decision. We had asked him to write either 'Yes' or 'No' in a secret corner of his next letter, and we were quite sure what the answer would be. How could anyone possibly refuse? We could hardly believe it when we saw '*NO!*' underlined in red. We waited, desperately, for his next visit, but we couldn't move him. However, having explained his reasons for wanting us to stay till we were a little older (something to do with the accommodation problem) he agreed to take us home for a fortnight if we dropped all postal threats, and if the Warden gave permission.

The Warden said that he was sorry, he'd like to oblige, but, for various reasons, holidays at home were not allowed. In many cases, he said, it was advisable to keep children as far from their home environment as possible. This, he admitted, didn't apply to our case, but he couldn't give preferential treatment. We were already being favoured by being allowed to write home once a week, whereas once a month was the general rule. This was quite enough for most of the orphans, who spent an agonised hour with a sheet of ruled paper, a scratchy pen, and a clogged bottle of ink, grinding out a month's coverage of the news, but my father had laid on an adequate supply of stationery and stamps, and he made such a fuss about the monthly ration that we were hastily allowed a weekly letter.

The real reason for the Warden's refusal to let us home, however, was the same as my father's. He thought that the return would unsettle us. We'd be better to stick it out, he said, till we were old enough to leave.

It was at this point that my father took the dog-eared *Plea* from his pocket and handed it to the Warden.

We didn't know what to do. After all the warnings about secrecy, after all the threats of what would happen to us if we were found out, he had deliberately thrown us to the wolves. (Literally, too; the Warden's name was Wolfe.) We bit our lips and stared at our feet as the pages rustled over. We didn't think we'd be punished there and then, but we expected the worst after our father was gone. Then, suddenly, we realised that the Warden was laughing. He folded up the *Plea*, which my father received with a certain amount of pride, came over to my brother and me, and knocked our heads together. 'Well,' he said, 'after that I think you deserve your holiday. On you go, before I change my mind.'

Contrary to what everybody expected, that fortnight didn't upset us at all. We seemed to settle down after it, having assured ourselves that the escape route was still open. And now, looking back, I realise that those years I protested against were some of the happiest of my life. Not because of the treats and celebrations which we looked forward to with perhaps more fervour than people outside the orphanage could understand, but because life was simple and uncomplicated.

There are times when some little thing, a trick of the light, a snatch of music or something even more nebulous can spark off a mood of delight which is almost ecstasy. The Aberlour environment fostered such feelings of pleasure which had nothing to do with the daily routine. I often had days when I waited, breathlessly, for something wonderful to happen. I could feel it, this heightened expectancy, this glorious event which lurked just out of sight. Most often, nothing did happen; but the feeling was there, the wish perhaps better than the fulfilment would have been.

There were other times more specifically happy. I can remember my thirteenth birthday, sitting on the porch at seven in the morning, waiting to go to Holy Communion. The sky was a deep and angry pink, the grass green as parsley, and crows drifted and cawed under the red clouds. That is one time when suddenly I *knew* I was happy; that, and another time, standing in the undertaker's yard (I can't think why I was there) watching him make a coffin large enough for a mother and two children to be buried together after dying in a burnt-out cottage. It was a sad occasion; and yet . . . it was a windy spring day, and life was glorious. And those winter afternoons, tramping home along the flint frozen roads, to our big steaming mugs of tea, and hunks of bread and jam—those were happy too.

Remembering that there was a depression going on outside, we at Aberlour, if we only realised it, were pretty well done by. Meals were plain but generous, we had a bed apiece with warm blankets and a heated dormitory, and there was plenty of hot water for baths. Pocket money was a penny a week (which was what I had been getting at home), and we had regular treats like dances and concerts and cinema shows.

Nevertheless, we were brought up to be sparing and economical with our resources, so that clothes were patched and darned, and even bootlaces had to be knotted together in several places before they could be replaced. Soap had to be used to the last sliver, and boots which were too small were taken back to be passed on to somebody else. But we didn't have the *worry* of poverty. Replacements were always forthcoming, with no effort on our part, so that many of us simply didn't know the value of money, and were apt to take things for granted.

On the other hand, we drifted easily into gratitude when

it was demanded of us. When one of the hyphenated land-owners in the district laid on a picnic, with footmen doling out pies and cakes and pitchers of cold fresh lemon, we cheered her dutifully but sincerely. I have since heard this type of woman described as a 'do-gooder'. That may well be, but to this day I remember the excitement of these picnics, and the wealth of goodwill they generated. We were content to receive the treats at their face value. If the donors really wanted thanks, they had only to look at our faces.

No doubt, in spite of our smiles, there was a certain look of pathos about us, because the orphanage, in 1929, was in many ways a rather Victorian establishment. The girls wore their long hair in plaits, and only on Sundays was it combed out and tied with a coloured ribbon. We wore pinafores all the time, and hard tackety boots which looked like government surplus. Our underwear was made on the premises from bales of cloth given to the orphanage or bought cheaply in bulk, so that a random check on a child might show a fawn-striped calico chemise, pink 'stays', butcher-blue knickers, a red flannel petticoat, and an orphanage dress so thick and heavy that it could double for an overcoat. In winter we were issued with 'flannels', peculiar short T-shaped garments which itched and tickled next to the skin, but once you got used to them it was possible to face any kind of weather.

If the girls looked dated, the boys were even more like those old sepia photographs in family albums. They, too, were dressed from bales of cloth bought in bulk. They wore short trousers and jackets with a square sailor collar, and the boys who were too old for sailor collars wore jackets with neither collars nor lapels, something like the kind the Beatles made popular. On Sundays they strangled in stiff white chokers. There was no uniform, as such, and use was made of any second-hand clothing handed in, but with so many garments made on the premises it was always

easy to pick out who was wearing orphanage issue. I dreaded
going into the standard orphan dress, buttoning at the back
with a half-belt, and made in hairy tweed in a vile khaki or
chocolate colour. For the first few months I peacocked about
in my very own clothes, but suddenly Matron pointed out
in a scandalised tone that my coat was 'right up to my
bottom' and that I would have to go up for a new one.

I was in despair. Now I would be dressed like any other
orphanage quean. I was looked over, my size guessed
roughly, and I was handed one in the current heathery-
coloured basket-weave tweed. If it hadn't been an orphanage coat, I felt, I would have rather liked it; and when
Sunday came, and I had walked about for half an hour in
the east wind, I had to admit that it was warmer and more
stormproof than anything I had ever worn. As my father
said, when he saw me wearing it, 'They didn't make a fool
of you with that coat.'

2

The first summer

DURING the summer we spent most of the time out of doors. We had no choice. Most of us had jobs of some kind to do, sweeping or dusting or washing dishes, but as soon as these were finished we were sent off to the playing fields, to get fresh air, and to keep us from getting under the Matron's feet.

The 'big' field was a rather uninviting area, full of clover and dockens and flowering grasses. Perhaps because the going was so heavy, I don't remember seeing anyone venture in for more than a few yards. It was enough to know that it was all ours, if we wanted. We preferred to stay in the 'wee' field, where four swings, two seesaws and a maypole were set out for our enjoyment.

The maypole had four loops of rope, rather like hang-men's nooses, which girls slipped round their waists and held while they ran round and launched themselves into space. As the maypole was on a slope, they could fly for quite a height. Getting a shot on the maypole called for a certain amount of influence. The loops were 'owned' by the girls who had managed to acquire the rope, and were lent only as a mark of great favour. I never aspired to owning, or even borrowing, a rope. The first time I was offered a shot, as a courtesy extended to a new girl, I tripped, skinned my legs and nearly choked myself. Next time, the iron ring at the top stuck, so that I wound myself smack round the pole, and ended up with a bruised face, and all the breath knocked out of my body.

The seesaws were equally masochistic, narrow planks on which we sat uncomfortably, and which went down with a thud which dirled our spines right up to the teeth. That left the swings. All my life I had coveted a swing, and now I found that if I bagged one after breakfast I was entitled to keep it for the rest of the day. I would sit for hours, listening to the bees and the crickets, and sucking a long stem of grass. Later on, I learned to swing standing up, going higher and higher till I was nearly over the bar, and eventually I learned how to jump off backwards. The girl who taught me that was a tinker, and no doubt had learned the trick at a fairground.

In a corner of the big field the older girls had gardens, little plots about the size of a hearthrug which they tended (or neglected) on their own. The keener ones harvested great crops of marigolds and cornflowers and poppies. But the favourite pastime was building 'wee hoosies'. It is amazing what can be done with some corrugated iron, a few old rugs, and some derelict furniture. I never owned a hoosie myself (like maypoles, they were status symbols), but I was once invited to tea in one, and had a most delicately served meal of rose-hips, clover heads, sourocks and sugarolly water!

Every afternoon there was a compulsory walk. If it was Sunday, or if we were going for an extra long distance, we were allowed to put our boots on, but mostly we got along on our bare feet. On very hot days our matrons were inclined to take us to the nearest convenient spot, and then leave us to explore or play on our own, and these explorations always ended in a search for food.

We ate everything we could lay our hands on, and quite a few things which should have poisoned us but didn't. We were chewing rose-hips long before rose-hip syrup was thought of, we ate handfuls of wood sorrel, and we picked thistles and ate the banana-like kernel under the prickles.

Beach nuts, hips and haws, grains of wheat and burdock stalks—we tried them all, and came to no harm. There was a tree in the drive which gave 'henny-yackles', a fruit like a cherry with a soft inside like pulpy apple. I have tried since to identify this fruit, but the best guess I can make is that it was a gean, or wild cherry.

Equally elusive was the bush which gave 'cough mixture' or 'nippies'. This is another plant I haven't seen since. It grew near the water, looked something like cow parsley, and had bunches of pods, like clumps of bananas, which tasted of liquorice or aniseed, and turned your teeth black if you ate too much.

But the best feasts came from the wild raspberries. They were everywhere, ripe and red and luxurious, and when we came home our pinafores were stained and we smelt like a jam factory. Later on there were blaeberries and brambles, and hardly a day passed without somebody knocking off a turnip from somebody's field. It wasn't that we needed the food, but our meals were so predictable, day after day, and we could not, like other children, run in at any old time and ask for a piece. What we ate probably did us less harm than a concentration of carbohydrate.

Occasionally, if Matron was in a good mood, we went for a hike, as opposed to an ordinary walk. This meant taking our tea with us, usually a better tea than if we had stayed at home. I remember one memorable slog over the moors. It sounds unbelievable, but we took our milk with us, in an open five-gallon can. We had to take it in turns to carry it, and through all the long miles we suffered the worry of keeping it unspilt. We dragged along over stones and rocks and heather, and by and by the word was passed along, 'We're going up the mountain. We're climbing Ben Rinnes.'

In some peculiar way this news helped to keep us going, as if we had been chosen for an Everest expedition. At least we would have something to show for our labours. No doubt we would be the first people to scale Ben Rinnes with five gallons of milk intact. The summit seemed miles away, but we kept at it grimly; and then, at the top, we straightened our backs, and paused to look at the view.

It was worth looking at. We stood at the top of a small ridge, and there, across the valley, cold and blue, with a glitter of streams flowing down its corries, was Ben Rinnes itself, incredibly high, with its plume of rock jagged and forbidding.

And then someone knocked over the milk can and we had nothing to drink.

I don't remember many wet days at Aberlour, but rain had to be very heavy to keep us in. If we didn't go for a walk we moped about, looking at dog-eared annuals, or dressing little bone dolls, and making the cupboard shelves into dolls' houses. One exceptionally wet Sunday we were issued with library books from some secret store. There wasn't time to read them through, and when they were gathered in at teatime they were stashed away and never brought out again. It was terribly frustrating. I was half-way through a real tear-jerker called *The Chorister Brothers,* all about two choirboys, one devout, the other very much a backslider who smoked instead of going to choir practice. The good one had just died, very affectingly, and his bad brother was making maudlin atonement at his grave, when the book was snatched away. I realised that it wasn't great literature, but I did want to know how it ended.

Every morning, at a quarter past seven, we went to church, over the little bridge, and past the graves where a few of the earlier orphanage children were buried. One girl, they said, had smiled in her coffin before it was screwed down, and they had put on the lid quickly because her smile was so awful; and round the corner was Canon Jupp, the Founder's grave, where his wife also lay buried. 'She did what she could', said the inscription—a rather mean measure of praise, I thought. But the churchyard was not

gloomy at this time of the morning. It was full of bird-song
and the scent of honeysuckle, and over a stile were the
church woods, slippery with pine needles, where you could
see rabbits and squirrels, and the peacocks on the lawn of
Aberlour House.

On Sunday nights, after Evensong, with incense and
candles and a procession, where we tried to make the choir-
boys laugh as they went down the aisle with their hymn-
books, there was an institution called 'Wolfie's Walk'. The
Warden, in his cassock, took the entire orphanage, except
the nursery babies, for a short circular walk. It was often
the only chance that brothers and sisters had to talk together, and it was very pleasant, strolling in the warm evening, between the green hedges and under the arching trees.
There was a running river of conversation, the crump of
hundreds of Sunday boots, and clouds of dust, as if a herd
of cattle were being rounded up. Down in the village the
smoke drifted lazily, and the village clock chimed a full
minute later than the orphanage one. We turned in at the
drive, past the blazing flower borders and the peppery smell
of lupins, and it was dark inside, dark and cool and rather
sad, after the dusty walk in the sunlight.

Six weeks after I arrived we went on our annual trip to
Lossiemouth.

On Lossie Day everything was rushed at in controlled
hysteria. Five minutes for breakfast, and no talking; ten
minutes to clear up, ten minutes to get ready for the train.
I don't know how we did it, but at ten to eight we were all
lined up at the front entrance, being briefed and inspected
before we set off on our adventure.

'Lossie' was definitely a dress occasion. Boots were worn
for the journey, with black stockings, Sunday coats, and
our red tams. These tams were a relic of the days when
orphans were orphans, and no nonsense. They had been
knitted in bulk, and no doubt in love, by some anonymous
benefactor, and were of a particularly lurid crimson, with

a large toorie on top, and the monogram AO in front. We wore them under protest, feeling branded and unbeautiful, and the only reason they didn't come to grief when we were out walking was that a lost tammie was apt to be replaced by one of even older vintage, threadbare and very well darned.

Anyway, there we were, five hundred of us, the big girls with their hair in ribbons, the youngsters in summer dresses, and the babies being counted over and over again by anxious nurses. Opposite stood the boys, all newly cropped heads and stiff collars, and among us moved the matrons, wearing posh new hats and comfortable old shoes, and poking us kindly with walking sticks.

A man in tweeds and pince-nez—the Headmaster I was told—watched indulgently with a band of teachers who couldn't resist coming, and all the domestic staff were present, dressed to kill, cooks, laundry maids, kitchen and dairy maids, gardeners, bootmenders, and the lame old man who delivered the letters. The nurses were unfamiliar in mufti, looking as if they had never prescribed castor oil in their lives, and the Warden's secretary carried a parasol and a prim black case, as if she were going to type letters on the train.

The Warden, his curly hair crinkling over his eyes, gave his pre-Lossie lecture, while we listened in impatient boredom. We were not in the mood for speeches. Then we started off, a long procession, with the orphanage dogs running alongside, down the leafy road to the village. All along the street, in the cool bright morning, neighbours came to their doors, and waved, and called, 'Aye, it's a rare day!' We poured into the station and into our special train, with the Spey prattling past only a few yards from the railway. The last dog was captured and handed in, the station master wiped his brow, and we yelled with excitement as the guard flagged us out.

I can remember only two things about the journey: the

tunnel, and the first sight of the sea. The tunnel ran through a rock near Craigellachie, and we were in complete blackness for only one second, but it was long enough to send half of us into hysterics. The sea came in sight at Elgin, and after that none of us could sit still. Soon after, the word 'Lossie' ran along the train in a great hiss, and we tumbled out, were pushed into some sort of order, and marched through the streets with our boots and our little calico bags called 'Lossie bags', and our tams all askew with excitement.

Lossiemouth had a salty, nautical air. We passed the harbour, narrow and horribly deep-looking, and fishermen in blue jerseys waved to us, and said, 'Aye? Back again?' The grass of the shore was wiry under our feet, with fawn sand at the roots, and the sea lost itself in a blue haze. In another ten minutes of magnificent organisation we entered a hall, took off our boots, hats and coats, while the boys lined up to have their chokers loosened, gave three cheers for Lossie, and assembled outside for the first of our three festive meals.

Food, I think, was in the hands of caterers, and was very unlike the routine orphanage fare. There was no V.I.P. treatment, no 'top table' for the élite. Everyone had the same rations: buns, pies, and lemonade drunk from the bottle. We wanted to prolong the meal, to 'miser' with the unaccustomed delicacies, but there was the seaside waiting to be explored, and there, edging in, were a dozen ice-cream carts with shaggy ponies and youths in white coats; all of them with their eyes on our Lossie bags, and our money, saved at a penny a week.

We all had our special penny; some of us had as much as two-and-sixpence, gifted by relatives and friends, but it was not the money that made our day. It was the sense of being on our own, to go where we liked, so long as we kept away from the town. The town, fortunately, did not tempt us. We had two miles of beach to roam, and a lighthouse

B

at the end of it, and that was as far as any child could
reasonably wish to go.

So we all dispersed, and spread out over the dunes, and
danced on the wet sand, and gathered pebbles, and
paddled, and wet the hems of our Sunday frocks. No one
bothered. The matrons were all away, having fly cups, we
suspected, in distant cafés. The sun shone, and we rushed
about madly, and returned at intervals to buy more sweets.
We wanted to do everything at once, but there was no time
to do anything at all. It was dinnertime already, and here
was the Warden trudging along the shore, blowing his
warning whistle.

Sausage rolls, buns, lemonade; the Headmaster drank
his virulent green tipple in academic joviality; the oldest
matron, tiny and spry, took a swig of gassy cola and
winked. We guzzled and burped, and spoke with our
mouths full, and our faces, already tanned, began to nip
afresh with sunburn. Behind a rock the tinies were being
'potted' one by one, and being shushed to sleep in the
shade; and not a crumb remained after the feeding of the
five hundred.

And now, with our first excitement quietened a little,
we were able to get down to things. Those who had
bathing suits went to bathe in little groups under carefully
picked swimmers, who showed off insufferably to the common paddlers at the edge. A few enthusiasts poked and
crawled about the rocks and came back with oozing Lossie
bags stuffed with buckies; and, with great determination,
a band of us set off on the annual pilgrimage to the lighthouse. It stood at the end of the bay, the last landmark
before the sand merged into sea and sky. It was like going
to the end of the world.

As it happened, very few of us reached the lighthouse.
Two miles was a long way in bare feet on a hot summer
day. The sea twinkled and danced, bright blue, the sand
shifted and hampering our walking; and then there were

so many distractions, a group of boys commandeering a
boat, with or without permission, two matrons on a sand-
dune, with a hankie over their knees, and a flask between
them—we knew they couldn't resist a fly cup; a man fishing,
who told us he'd caught six salmon and a shark; and our
black Pomeranian, Nigger, appearing from nowhere, and
seeming surprised when we flung ourselves on him in
ecstasy.

These interruptions all took time, and the lighthouse
seemed to recede like a mirage as we struggled through the
sand with the desperation of Foreign Legion survivors. At
last, however, we reached it, slightly surprised, and very
much awed. It was so much bigger than the chalk stroke
it had appeared from the train, and it did not stand with its
feet in the sea, nor did it mark the end of the land. The
coast curved on to Hopeman and Burghead, and we
winced through rough grass and gazed up at the big white
tower.

The keeper, on the gallery, hollered, 'Are ye comin' up?'
and we bawled back, 'Yes, sir!' in our best institutional
Scots. Then we found the door and began to climb.

A hundred and forty-five steps, I think. At first we whispered in reverence, then we giggled as we went round and
round, and then we needed all our breath for climbing.
The stone was cool on our feet, and everything beautifully
clean.

Suddenly we were out in the fresh air. We weren't sure
that we liked it. The sea seemed paler and more vast, the
sand shaded back into grass and houses, and the breeze
was cool and strong. Suppose, just suppose the rail gave
way . . . a gull swerved by, level with our faces, and we all
went in to see the lantern, and pretended to understand all
about oil and reflectors and candle-power and revolutions.
To us it was just a marvellous golden thing under a glass
dome.

Now we could say we had seen the lighthouse, but the

green was very far away, and we were beginning to feel
hungry again. As we trailed back we saw the Warden blowing his whistle for tea, with Spey, his black Labrador, by his
side. This was his second trek along the shore. 'Aye, you've
a big heart!' a visitor once said to him, hearing that he
intended to set five hundred children free on a beach, and
round them up again for every meal. His whistling system
sounded crazy and ineffectual, but it always worked. No
one was late, no one went missing, but no doubt his feet
ached badly after Lossie!

If we looked tired when we queued up for tea the matrons
looked rested, serene and content, as if they enjoyed getting away from us for a while. This time there were urns of
tea lined up, and we sipped with an air of leisure. We were
not to wander away again. We played quietly in the evening
light, till it was time to put on our boots and stockings, again,
and then the last rite of Lossie was enacted. We all filed
past to receive the traditional bar of chocolate, a tuppeny
bar, almost too valuable to eat.

After that it was time to go home. Our coats were
crumpled, our tams cocked at an outrageous angle, and
our Lossie bags bumped and bulged against our hips. We
went through the clean streets with a noise like a river, and
it was heartbreaking to go. Every window was thrown up,
every doorway filled, and voices called, 'Haste ye back, noo!
See ye next year!' The youngest baby was fast asleep in the
Warden's arms, cuddled in to his neck, and the oldest
matron urged on her five-year-olds, 'Come on now, bairnies,
hurry on. My, you'll a' sleep the night!'

Horror at the station! Nigger, our Pomeranian, was
lost! Rags, the fox terrier, was with the senior boys, and
Spey had seen everyone safely on to the train. But Nigger
—no, there he was! A snapping, snarling bundle, he was
handed in and held fast as the platform glided away and
left Lossie behind for another year.

We sang all the way home, which was very courageous

of us, considering that Lossie was over, and that, with a
few minor exceptions, we had nothing to look forward to
till Christmas. Of course, we still had our chocolate, and the
buckies, now beginning to smell a little. Tomorrow we might
coax Cook into boiling them, and we would eat them in
corners, very delicately, from the point of a pin; but tomorrow was bleak, the morning after, the terrible anti-
climax.

But we sang, and screamed again in the tunnel, and looked
with disfavour on the swift river and the blue ridge of Ben
Rinnes. The square was golden, the whole village golden
in the slanting sun, and the orphanage was like a cloister,
cool, quiet, and incredibly dim after a day of sea glare. A
gong rang in the distance, and we filed into the dining hall
for bread and butter and mugs of milk under the stags'
heads and the painting of the Founder.

And that was the end of it; sand between our toes, our
buckies dumped in the bath—'You're not taking those to
bed with you!'—and sticky faces hastily wiped and snuggled
down. It had been a rare day. It always was a rare day for
Lossie; and before the Matron came round with her keys
to lock the front door, before her footsteps dwindled away
down the corridor, we were drifting away on soft surges of
sleep, and turning round, round, in a golden lantern under
the sky.

3

The dark of winter

FROM the very beginning of our orphanage life we were made to realise that we had to be self-reliant. We made our own beds, cleaned our own boots, and in some cases we had to darn the boys' stockings as well.

At the age of ten or thereabouts we were deemed old enough to take our share in the daily chores. At this point, jobs were more or less voluntary. One somewhat retarded girl of about twelve spent her spare time patching sheets, and there were a few dedicated cleaners who liked nothing better than to whisk a broom or flourish a duster. I was in no hurry to patch or do anything else. All I wanted was peace to read; but Miss Rae, our matron, decided that all this reading was a form of laziness. As from Monday, I was informed, I would be in charge of the courtyard passage, and I would hold the job for a fortnight.

No one could say I wasn't willing. I swept till the dust blinded me, I dusted the panelling and shook the door-mat over myself and anyone else in sight. On Saturdays I knelt with a fellow serf and scrubbed the stone floor from one end to the other, looking typically orphan in a sack apron, and dragging a heavy zinc pail behind me. At the end of that fortnight I was as sick of that passage as the Matron was of me. I can remember her standing over me in a black-and-white plaid frock, a white-haired woman with a kindly face and a shrill, fierce voice.

'You'll never make a worker, lassie!' she scolded, shaking her head at me. 'You're that *awkward*-looking. I've nae time for left-handed scrubbers.'

The Wife, as Miss Rae was called (I never found out why), never did come to terms with my reading, my scrubbing, or my left-handedness. Jeannie, the patcher of sheets, was much nearer her ideal. When *she* wasn't sewing she brandished a very efficient scrubbing brush in her *right* hand; and yet, when it was time for me to move up to another dayroom, the Wife suddenly and shamefacedly presented me with a hair clasp of the kind that I had coveted for months.

'You canna read with your hair over your eyes like that,' she scolded, pushing me away before I could thank her.

The scrubbing episode, though tackled eagerly enough, intensified my homesickness. Before coming to the orphanage I had been a reasonably promising scholar, encouraged by my teachers, entering musical festivals with my brother, and once even winning a prize for elocution. Now this was all in the past. The elocution was even a drawback. One of the worst things an orphan could do, apparently, was to 'talk posh'. It looked as if I was going to grow into a straw-sucking illiterate or a domestic drudge.

What was wrong, of course, was that the school holidays had lasted too long. The matrons were beginning to think so too. One morning there was a hideous jangle from the bell tower. The staff sighed blissfully, and we flocked up the school brae in clean pinafores, and left the buildings silent for the first time in weeks.

St. Margaret's, as well as being the orphanage school, in our own grounds, was the Episcopal school for the district, and a family of railway children cycled in from Craigellachie every day. On the face of it, they might have been better off in the village, because our school was only a junior secondary, and, like the orphanage, run on very frugal lines. Slates, believe it or not, were still in use in the lower classes, and when we graduated to jotters we had to fold each page down the middle, and use both sides.

Pencils were chopped in two, and issued only on the pro-
duction of the previous tiny stub; but there was a cosiness,
an intimacy about the place which made up for the lack
of amenities.

Going to school made life normal again for me; and
autumn brought other comforts. Choir practices started,
and Leonard was roped in as a soloist. The Warden's wife
inaugurated a Brownie Pack, and I was made a second in
the Gnomes. To crown everything, I had a poem in the
orphanage magazine.

The monthly magazine was a blue-covered booklet with
a panoramic drawing of the orphanage on the back cover,
and on the front the picture of a child holding a man's
hand, looking up at him soulfully, and saying :

> 'Protect me, ye of larger growth.
> Hear my appeal. Please take my hand
> And lead me safely through the days
> Of childhood into grown-up land.'

It was a verse we did not entirely relish.

The subscription for this monthly bulletin was a shilling
a year, and a very well spent shilling it was. Apart from the
business contents, a *Wants* column—'Rolls of flannel for
undergarments, girls' liberty bodices, lads' working boots,
etc.'—it had a fascinating journal, written by the Warden
himself, a simple day-to-day account of orphanage happen-
ings. There was also a popular and very revealing feature
called 'Old boys' and girls' letters' which gave a clear in-
sight into what Aberlour meant to those who had left.
The letters mirrored success, or showed nostalgia, depend-
ence, gratitude or despair. Some were cleverly and smartly
written, others were ground out with difficulty, the grammar non-existent, but the message perhaps coming over
more clearly because of that. Most people read the letters
before anything else.

It was the magazine which was to set me off on a literary career.

I had always wanted to be a writer. I can remember the exact moment of making the decision, when I was seven years old, reading Arthur Mee's *Children's Encyclopædia* on a rainy day. I had filled notebooks with epics like *From Stone Age to Civilisation*, which always seemed to fizzle out with the dinosaurs. Now I decided to tackle something simpler, and, swayed by Brownie enthusiasm, I wrote a short poem about fairies which I decline to quote here. After a token protest I allowed someone to show it to the Warden, with the introduction, 'Please, sir, Dorothy Haynes has written a poingtry.' He looked it over, nodded vaguely, tucked the paper in his pocket, and went away down the passage.

Although at this stage I was still a fairly new girl, I had already noted a number of points about C. A. E. Wolfe. 'Wolfie', as I might as well call him now, was in his thirties, a pleasant, rather stocky man with dark curly hair. He was kindly, shrewd, and always surrounded by children—he had a son and daughter of his own. He made great play with his name—'I'm the big bad Wolfe' and so on—and he seemed to have the idea that he really did possess some vulpine qualities, such as the ability to prowl silently and pounce on unsuspecting wrongdoers. Nobody ever told him (or perhaps he knew, after all) that in fact his chances of catching anyone out were slim. For one thing, he liked the sound of his own voice, which was loud, jovial and English; for another, he always went about in a haze of pipe smoke; and, thirdly, like a shadow before him went Spey, his black Labrador.

Over the years Wolfie had at least four Speys, but they have all melted into one legendary animal with a wonderful repertoire of tricks. Spey always led the choir procession in church, he could distinguish between Matins and Choral Eucharist, and (so Wolfie said) he would snore

if a sermon lasted longer than ten minutes. Now he served
as a useful early warning system. Nobody was ever up to
mischief when the Warden appeared. We were all busy
stroking and fondling Spey.

But there was one more thing I had noticed about Wolfie.
Kind, genial, efficient he might be, but he was also absent-
minded. He frequently forgot our pocket money, he had to
be reminded about appointments, and if he stuffed things
into his pockets they were as good as lost. And there he
was, ambling up the corridor with my poem.

I ran after him. 'Please, sir, can I have my poem back?'

'Your . . . oh, your poem!' He made no move to look
for it. 'I'll give it to you later. I want to print it in the
magazine.'

I didn't answer. Delight takes one like that sometimes.

'I'll put "by Dorothy Haynes" on it. Would you like that?'

'Yes, sir.' He was off again, his mind on his next job,
when I ran after him and tugged at his coat-tails. 'Please,
sir . . .' My face was hot and scarlet. 'Please, sir, would
you put "Dorothy K. Haynes"?'

He laughed. 'All right,' he said, and patted my shoulder.
I swaggered back to my dayroom. How great, I thought,
is the status that authorship conveys!

I hadn't the sense to be modest about it. 'Are you *glad*
you're getting your poem in the magazine?' somebody
asked suspiciously, and I said yes, of course I was. I shouldn't
have done that. It was too cocky. I should have pretended
reluctance, hung my head and scraped my toes and pleaded
for anonymity.

But I didn't; and I got my reward when at last the
magazine appeared. There was the poem all right, but
not the literary signature I had been promised. Under-
neath was the damning statement, 'By Brownie Haynes,
age 11.'

Still, it was a start.

Perhaps because of the publicity of my poem, but more

likely, I am inclined to think, because I had extra pocket money of my own, I found myself with an inseparable friend.

There were quite a few girls that I liked, and with whom I was on pleasant terms, but I had never yet had a special chum. Chums' names were linked together, they walked arm in arm, they whispered secrets, and they shared everything; and Meta Morrison, out of the blue, announced that she and I were chums.

Meta had metallic-looking blonde hair, a sallow skin, and cold, glittery grey eyes. There was something hard, something ruthless, about her, but she smarmed up to me, mesmerised me with that cold grey glitter, and gave me a ha'penny cake of toffee. Obediently, without even liking her very much, I accepted her advances. Next week it was my turn to share my pocket money, and because I had money left in charge for me, doled out at threepence a week, Meta netted three halfpence.

We didn't have much in common. We mooned about, and Meta recounted to me interminable letters she said she'd received, in which she'd been promised astonishing presents, from jumper suits to cases of oranges and leather leggings. The leggings especially featured in every conversation. Why she wanted them so much I don't know, nor can I imagine what they would have looked like over her tackety boots, but she seemed to have an obsession about them.

She had another obsession which affected me more directly. She could never get enough to eat.

By this time, she had stopped sharing her weekly penny, and was taking the bigger part of my threepence—not only what I gave her in cash, but a share of what I bought for myself. Now she wanted my meals as well.

The giving away or accepting of other people's food was forbidden, but it could be done, with a little ingenuity. We would crouch over our soup or porridge bowls, and then, when the Lady Superintendent, or whoever was in charge of the dining hall went past, there would be a quick exchange, a full basin for an empty one, and the furtive crouch would be resumed. Meta accounted for quite a lot of my rations in this way, and on top of that I was expected to 'pooch' or pocket bread for her.

Here I was breaking another rule. Food had to be consumed at the table, but there was a certain charm in nibbling a crust or a biscuit out of hours. We smuggled things out by hiding them under our pinafores, and sidling out with our hands clasped demurely over the lump.

Meta got my breakfast scone, my chunk of bread which was supposed to clean my soup bowl for my pudding, and at least a slice of my bread at teatime. She guzzled all my biscuits, my cheese or hard-boiled eggs, and on Wednesdays a good slab of my steamed pudding as well. Heaven only knows what had come over me. I grudged her the food; I had a healthy appetite myself, and I had always looked forward to biscuit nights; but if Meta didn't get her due, she sulked, and I couldn't stand the atmosphere. Next time I would slip in a bit extra, and she'd slide her arm into mine, and promise me a shot of her leggings when they arrived.

The clock was changed, the dark nights came, and gases were lit in the dayrooms. Meta and I sat together, her jaws going munch, munch on my jammy crusts, while I licked my lips, and pretended not to be hungry, and listened to the girls singing.

> 'I am a poor wee orphanage girl,
> My mother she is dead,
> My father he is far away
> And cannot buy me bread.
> Alone I stand at the window
> To hear the church bells ring,
> God bless my dear old mother,
> She's dead and in her grave.
> Ding, dong, my castle bell!

> Farewell, my mother !
> Bury me in the old churchyard
> Beside my eldest brother. . . .'

We always sang in the evenings. The gases burned green,
the black windows showed nothing but our own scared re-
flections, and our songs were about fearful things, as we got
on with our eternal mending. Our hands were muffled in
long black stockings, our darning needles flicked silver, and
one song followed another as the gas hissed and the fire
died down towards eight o'clock.

> 'My parents gave me good learning,
> Good learning they gave to me.
> They sent me down to a butcher's shop,
> A butcher's boy to be.
>
> I fell in love with a nice young girl,
> With a dark and a rolling eye,
> And she promised for to marry me
> In the month of sweet July.
>
> We walkèd east, and we walkèd west,
> And we walkèd along the shore,
> Till at last I took my knife from my belt,
> And I stabbed her to the core.'

We did not pause in our darning. The knitting women
at the guillotine could not have been more intent. We were
not consciously miserable in our singing, but we could not
get away from blood and grief.

> 'But something wi' ma hert gaed wrang.
> A vessel burst, and blood outsprang.
> My days on earth will no' be lang,
> For noo's my time, and I maun gang.'

By this time, we had worked ourselves into a fine emotional mood. Ham actors, the lot of us, we sang on our
knees, our hands stretched out appealingly.

> 'There are many, sad and weary,
> In this pleasant world of ours,
> Crying every night so sadly,
> "Won't you buy my pretty flowers?" '

These songs, of course, were not peculiar to the orphanage. They crop up in various guises, all over the country.
But the ones that were handed down to us were invariably
sad and violent, usually rounding themselves off with
murder.

> 'I stabbed her and stabbed her
> Till the blood did o'erflow,
> And buried her body
> In the valley below.'

And, for sheer haunting inanity,

> 'Last night in Tokyo
> I met a man without a toe.
> His toe was sore, he cried no more,
> Last night in Tokyo.'

The reason for this preoccupation with death and dying
lay, I think, in our collective past. Our music was just what
one would expect from deprived and cloistered humanity.
Even the more fortunate children were influenced by
something beyond them, some mass memory which brought
to their minds terrors they had never known. What of the
girl who was admitted to the orphanage under a year old,
but who, at seven, swore that she had seen a public hanging at Aberdeen? She was not an imaginative child, and

she never became much of a reader, but she knew how a man would look on the gallows, the blue tongue, the twitching limbs, and the crowd watching in sick lust and excitement.

Then there was the pathetic child who was supposed to be backward, but who was only scholastically retarded, because she was deaf and half-blind. She told us, meekly, that a stepmother had stuck a needle in her eyes, and poured boiling oil in her ears. Was she pulling our legs, or was there a dormant memory of storied atrocities?

> 'Then up and spake her cruel step minnie,
> "Tak' ye the burnin' lead. . . ." '

We did not know, but when she was once asked to sing on her own she confounded us by piping, in a very sweet voice, a gentle little lyric by Blake.

> 'I have no name,
> I am but two days old.
> What shall I call thee?
>
> Pretty Joy,
> Joy is my name.
> Sweet Joy befall thee.'

We did not approve of this high-falutin' stuff at all. What we wanted was the thrill and the terror, the whispered recounting of orphanage lore. An icy moon frosted the windows, and the brass endowment plates over our beds gleamed wanly. Happed and cosy in scarlet blankets, we shuddered at what might appear to us.

We had good reason to fear hauntings. Had not a ghost appeared in the time of the Founder? I quote here from a statement by Canon Jupp, in writing, after he had spent

a night sleeping in the children's dormitory, having given
up his room to a visitor.

'As near as I can tell, I fell asleep about eleven o'clock,
and slept very soundly for some time. I suddenly awoke
without any apparent reason, and felt an impulse to turn
round, my face being towards the wall from the children.
Before turning I looked up and saw a soft light in the room.
The gas was burning low in the hall, and the dormitory
door being open, I thought it probable that the light came
from that source. It was soon evident, however, that such
was not the case. I turned round, and then a wonderful
vision met my gaze. Over the second bed from mine, and
on the same side of the room, was floating a small cloud
of light, forming a halo of the brightness of the moon on
an ordinary moonlight night.

'I sat upright in bed, looked at this strange appearance,
took up my watch and found the hands pointing to five
minutes to one. Everything was quiet, and all the children
sleeping soundly. In the bed over which the light seemed
to float slept the youngest of the six children mentioned
above (recently admitted to the orphanage on the death of
their mother). I asked myself, "Am I dreaming?" No! I
was wide awake. I was seized with a strong impulse to rise
and touch the substance, or whatever it might be (for it
was about five feet high), and was getting up when something seemed to hold me back. I am certain I heard nothing, yet I felt and perfectly understood the words, "No, lie
down, it won't hurt you." I at once did what I was told to
do. I fell asleep shortly afterwards, and rose at half past
five, that being my usual time.

'At six o'clock I commenced dressing the children, beginning at the bed furthest from the one in which I had
slept. Presently I came to the bed over which I had seen
the light hovering. I took the little boy out, placed him
on my knee, and put on some of his clothes. The child had
been talking with the others, suddenly he was silent. And

then looking at me hard in the face with an extraordinary expression, he said, "Oh! Mr. Jupp, my mother came to see me last night. Did you see her?" For a moment I could not answer the child. I then thought it better to pass it off, and said, "Come, we must make haste, or we shall be late for breakfast." '

Whispering this tale, we all agreed that we would prefer our parents, however much they had been loved, not to appear to us thus. And yet we loved the idea of fear and horror. We shuddered deliciously as we expounded the myth of the midnight prowler.

We were not supposed to mention him. The authorities insisted that he did not exist, but the rumours were tenacious and convincing. He stood at the beds, he glided between the gas jets, and he left red finger-marks on the walls. One night he came to the dormitory and whispered into the dark, 'Who wants bread and jam? Come on, bonnie lassies, who wants bread and jam?' At first the girls jeered and repulsed him, but after a time the soft voice tempted them. One girl crept to the window and slid her hand under the sill, and the moon shone on the red, juicy piece in her hand; but when she put it in her mouth she spat it out and screamed, 'You big devil, that's not bread and jam! *It's bread and flesh!*'

Was this a dressed-up travesty of Holy Communion, or did it hark back to even older rites? All we knew was that it brought a coldness to our cheeks, so that we grued in the gaslight; and down the corridor the working girls, privileged to sit up a little later, sang as they sewed their 'fine seams', the clothes they would take with them when they went out to service.

> 'Oh I had a lover in Glasgow,
> And I had a lover in Dundee,
> And I had a lover in Americky,
> And that's the one that ruined me!

First he took me to Glasgow,
And then he took me to Dundee,
And then he took me to Americky,
And left me with a baby on my knee.'

I think they sang that in all innocence. Certainly we
younger ones had no idea why Matron snapped, 'That'll do
now, girls. We'll have no more of that.' But . . . how many
of us were sure of our legitimacy? How many of the singers,
with their long hair and pinafores, would face life later on,
with the same plaint on their lips? Loneliness, ignorance,
the pull of heredity—the cards were stacked against some
of us before we started.

For the moment we were safe, but we did not trust our
safety. The gas flared, it was time to put away our mending,
and go down the dark passages to bed, under the fishtail
burners, in and out of the pools of shadow; and late at
night, when the matrons had gone to their rooms, and the
doors were locked, so that we couldn't escape, Miss McKee,
the Lady Superintendent, would pace the corridors, turning out the gases, one by one—how did we *know* it was
Miss McKee? And what would happen when the last jet
dwindled to black? Someone with black gloves would go
creep, creep, turning the gases on again, but *not lighting
them*. . . .

'Oh—!
I want to go home!
I want to go home!
I'm nae gonnie stay in the orphanage no more,
The place where the matrons are always indoor.
Take me over the sea.
The matron'll never catch me.
Oh my, I think I shall die
If you don't *take me home*!'

The desire to go home was strong even in the children who had no suitable home to go to. Meta was always romancing about it. 'I got another letter today. They're coming for me next month. I've to be measured for a coat to go away in. . . .'

And then one evening Meta did go away, but not officially. She ran away after school.

I knew nothing about it. I had never suspected. All I knew was that before tea there was an air of excitement and suspense, whispers in corners, and sly nods and nudges. It wasn't till we were lined up for tea that somebody burst out with the news. Three girls were missing, and one was Meta Morrison.

As we gabbled and speculated, over our bread and marge, I chewed quietly, not quite sure how I felt about things. Meta was away. There was a great singing relief in my heart—and in my stomach. Everything on my plate belonged to me! And yet I knew that it wouldn't last. Girls had run away before, and been brought back before they'd covered a few miles. I was hurt, too, at not being taken into Meta's confidence. I wouldn't have gone with her—I just wasn't the type for this sort of escapade, even if I'd expected it to work—but at least she might have consulted me. That's what friends were for.

Nobody questioned me. Nobody even suspected me of being implicated. We savoured our mugs of hot tea, and the yellow shine from the gas globes. Somewhere, out in the wet and blowy dark, the absconders were trudging along —we pictured them sleeping under hedges, and roasting rabbits and salmon over gypsy fires. Not one of us but hoped they would make a go of it.

They didn't, of course. They were in bed, in disgrace, when we came out of the hall. A loud and dramatic wailing came from the dormitory, but we were forbidden to go in. The wicked ones were not to be allowed the luxury of an audience.

Naturally, a few of us nipped in as soon as Matron's back was turned. Soon a message was sent to me that Meta wanted me, and at once.

Promptly, but reluctantly, I entered the bedroom. Meta was gulping and sobbing, with an odd choking moan for good measure. I couldn't see in the darkness, but I bent over her, and asked what was wrong.

'I'm hungry,' she said. 'Where's my bread?'

I hadn't been prepared for this. 'I—I ate it,' I stuttered, 'I thought . . .'

The sobbing stopped. She banged up in bed and pushed her face towards me. 'You're a rotten greedy pig! You were supposed to pooch bread for me. I *told* you! I told you!'

I should have broken with her there and then, but, amazingly, I didn't. I apologised. I promised her *all* my pocket money next day, and the following morning I was back to the old routine, getting hungrier and hungrier as the days wore on.

Gradually, I learned what had happened to the runaways. They told the tale with pride, and no doubt a certain amount of embellishment. They had decided to cut across the moors to Dufftown (though what they expected to do when they got there was anyone's guess), but after two miles, when they came to Craigellachie, they were both wet and hungry They climbed a flight of stairs to a large house, knocked at the door, and told the lady who answered that they had no food and no money.

The lady, who saw orphanage children every week, noted the pinafores under the coats, the tackety boots, and the peculiar orphanage intonation, but she gave no sign of recognition.

'Oh dear,' she said, 'you'd better come in and get warm. Would you like a cup of tea?'

It is here, I suspect, that romance took over a little. The girls were led into a lamplit room with a blazing fire, velvet armchairs, and fur rugs. Fish and chips appeared, and if the plates weren't silver, the tea-service was. Over cakes and chocolate biscuits, confidences were exchanged. 'Yes, we're running away from the orphanage. Oh, they're cruel to us there! We have to go to bed at eight o'clock, and we get black marks if we don't behave. . . .'

While they were at their third cup of tea their hostess went out for more milk, and telephoned the Warden in passing.

The Warden, they said, was blazing angry ('in a right tight birr' was the actual phrase), not only because of the worry they had caused, but because of the trouble they had given to outsiders. A mile from Aberlour he stopped the car, ordered them on to the roadside, and gave them their choice. 'Do you want to sleep here in the ditch, or come back to your warm bed? It's up to you.'

They plumped for the warm bed. Oddly enough, they bore the Warden no grudge for capturing them, nor for the punishment they received later. Nor did they hold their hostess's behaviour against her. It was a dirty trick, they agreed, but she had been good to them. It would be a long time before they would forget the fish and chips.

I could have done with some fish and chips myself, after hearing all that. Meta's appetite was as insatiable as ever. Then one day I came home from school to find that she had left, in a taxi. No one told me where she had gone. All I could think of was the fact that now my meals were my own. I gorged happily for a week or so, till someone remarked that I looked a lot happier since Meta had gone. That did it. It all came out in a great gust of hatred and relief. The dayroom listened with fascination, and then delivered their verdict.

'You're daft,' they said.

4

The good times

WINTER at the orphanage, however, was by no means all gloom. There was something about the Speyside air, the tangy pine scent, the cold mountain freshness, which made us wake bright and avid for every new day. The thick navy knickers, the long black stockings, the bulky petticoats, and, above all, the 'flannels', made us impervious to the worst the weather could do.

In winter our healthy appetites doubled. At first I had choked and gagged over my porridge, and found the scone which followed too dry to swallow. Now I found myself looking forward to breakfast. The porridge was milled from our own oats, the milk came from our own farm, and no breakfast since has tasted better than that hot creamy bowlful. The scones, too, became an obsession. They were soft and slightly sweet, and once you were used to them you couldn't get enough.

On Wednesdays we had slabs of dumpling instead of milk pudding, huge chunks of clootie dumpling which swelled us out so that we felt heavy and lethargic all afternoon. But Friday, dietetically, was the day of days. Instead of soup, which was filling and nourishing, but nevertheless just soup, we had mince and potatoes. It is quite impossible to explain how much we looked forward to 'mince and tatties' day. The dinner was made to institutional standards, the potatoes boiled in their jackets, and the mince thickened with oatmeal, but we wouldn't have changed it for boar's head or roast peacock. We scraped up every morsel until

our basins shone, and next Friday was a whole long week
away.

Winter brought snow, nothing like the stained, messy
stuff which fouls the streets in towns. Aberlour snow lay
pure and white till it melted, and then the slush ran in
quick runnels down the long hills till the Spey burst its
banks and roared yellow and steaming under the bridges.
Aberlour snow fell overnight, heavily and completely, so
that we woke to a luminous lightness, an extravagant
transformation with all the trees muffled to twice their size,
and lawns and pathways smoored into one gorgeous level
of white.

Standing at the dayroom window, our hands on the hot
radiator, we watched the raspberry-streaked sky turn to a
blaze of sun. And then, plunging and tossing, the farm
horses, Yorkie and Prince, galloped past, all jingling and
musical, dragging the snow-plough, a great white wave
shearing to each side. Up past the school it went, and soon,
through the gaps in the houses, we could see them spanking
along the village street, *our* plough, *our* horses, still fresh
and frisky, up the big drive and past again !

There was never any nonsense about putting down grush
at the orphanage drives. Once the snow had fallen, it lay,
white and starchy, ready for sliding and sledging. We made
glassy black slides down the school brae, for what seemed
to be days at a time; but, best of all, there was the sledging.

The girls were poor relations in the matter of sledges.
We had one between thirty; but the boys, able to fiddle
wood and iron, and commandeer tools, seemed to have one
apiece. No matter; they were willing to share, and there was
a network of long, steep, winding braes, just perfect for
sledging. We could rush downhill for nearly a mile at a
time, face down, doing dreadful things to the toes of our
boots as we steered. Sometimes the Subwarden, in cordu-
roy breeches, condescended to let a girl share his toboggan.
He took me, and halfway down we swerved to avoid a

vacant-looking boy maundering up on the wrong side of the track. The sledge hit a tree and splintered, the tree was badly scarred, but we were both thrown clear, into a snowdrift. It's amazing how angry the clergy can get without actually swearing.

November brought Guy Fawkes' night, and the bonfire. During the thirties neither bonfires nor fireworks had much of a vogue in Scotland. The odd sparkler or Roman candle marked the date, but firework displays were left to the English or the impossibly affluent.

And to Aberlour Orphanage. We made the Fifth a night to remember.

Our arangements were as sensible as could be devised. Our bonfire was enormous, trees, furniture, tar-barrels, and a guy, but it was roped off, and we watched it from a very respectful distance. Fireworks—and we had a magnificent display, bangers, rockets, Catherine wheels, the lot—were entirely in the hands of the Warden and the housemasters. The village children massed enviously beyond the field, the locals couldn't resist coming, but *no one* was allowed beyond the barrier. And no one was ever hurt.

I think there was a Guy Fawkes' Dance. Certainly there was a dance for Hallowe'en, with plenty of ducking for apples, and a Founder's Day dance on December 11th, and a dance on the Warden's birthday. Our own birthdays we celebrated with a holiday from school, an exemption from work, a penny, and permission to spend any money we had saved down the village. There was also the chance, too, that the Warden might be going somewhere in his car, in which case he would stop and shout, 'Anybody got a birthday today?'

But through the length of winter, the good times and the bad, Christmas shone like a beacon.

I don't know what I expected an orphanage Christmas to be like. Christmas Day in the workhouse, probably. They would do their best, but it wouldn't be like home. It couldn't be.

This was where I was wrong. My first Christmas at Aberlour was a revelation to me.

The excitement began in early December, when conferences were held about decorations. This was a matter which was always taken seriously. The matrons were given an allowance for the usual paper chains, and a certain amount of holly-stealing was winked at, but neither the money nor the holly stretched far enough, so their savings were squandered on items like frost and tinsel and balloons, and the infirmary dispensed more cotton wool in December than in all the rest of the year.

The 'printings', however, were the children's own contribution to the Christmas décor, and they kept us quiet for hours. We sat at the tables with large sheets of drawing paper and new pencils, and after much measuring and gnawing we printed and coloured seasonal greetings in large, snow-covered capitals. The messages were not original—GOD BLESS THE WARDEN, or A MERRY CHRISTMAS TO ALL —but originality was not the aim. What mattered most was that the colours should be bright, and that in the most conspicuous place should hang the prince of printings, A MERRY CHRISTMAS TO OUR BENEFACTORS. We never quite knew who our benefactors were, but we suspected they must be among the huntin' and shootin' types who came around occasionally, and exclaimed about how *well* we looked, and who 'enriched our dietary', as the Warden put it, with salmon and grouse and other things which we never really appreciated. We did not mind paying lip-service to these nebulous friends of ours. It was Christmas time, and we greeted them magnanimously, tweeds, English accents, and all.

So we went on with our printing and preparations, and the days before Christmas passed in delicious torment. We all knew what treats to expect. Orphanage Christmases

ran true to form. But in spite of the promises of parties and
fun everyone wondered, a little wistfully, will there be
something special for me? Something from outside, a letter,
a card, even, to show off and put on the mantelshelf? Nearly
every child had *someone* to send something, but the unlucky ones hoped in the face of despair, and kept on hoping
until Christmas was well over.

I didn't know what to do about hanging up a stocking.
Would it be all right? I asked, half expecting to be laughed
at, but everyone assured me that my stocking would be
filled. It was, too. An apple, an orange, a cake of chocolate and a penny may not seem much today but it meant a
great deal to orphanage children forty years ago. We
wakened in the small hours and scoffed the lot, and hid the
peel and cores under the pillows; then, at half past six, just
dropping off to sleep, we were wakened so that the older
girls could go to Holy Communion.

It was an unfortunate thing, but our Christmas worship
tended to be overshadowed by our Christmas meals. They
knelt in the whispering church, with the lovely words of
the Liturgy muttering up in the chancel, and all they could
think of was breakfast. Instead of the usual porridge we
were to have bread, tea and sausages and they fidgeted desperately until the Blessing was over and they were free to go.

After polishing off the sausages with our queer little
wooden-handled forks, and nibbling the chocolate Santas
our matron had put by our plates, we should have been
able to concentrate on the service at eleven o'clock; and
indeed we did enjoy it, with the choir in their crackling
clean surplices, and the Christmas hymns triumphant from
the packed pews; but by this time we were beginning to
think about dinner, and Christmas dinner was one of the
highlights of the day.

In an effort to make it as festive as possible, the small
boys dined with the little girls at the East Block, while the
older girls were invited by the boys to the famous

McCorquodale dining hall. This hall, the largest in the north
of Scotland, had an almost baronial atmosphere. Stags'
heads looked down from the panelled walls on an immense
parquet floor, and down the length of the floor were long,
long tables, covered, for this once, with tablecloths. A
special table was set for the Warden and any important
guests, and it was fascinating to see them eating orphanage
fare and enjoying it so much. To our mind, the lip-smack-
ing and eye-rolling was just a little overdone.

Grace was a tiresome preliminary, as we squinted at each
other's basins to make sure no one had more than their
share. The first course was stew, a peculiar beef stew with
a suspicion of venison and plenty of thick floury gravy. The
clashing of spoons and forks made the hall sound like a
battlefield, then the puddings were carried in, with much
steam and cheering. Large slices were slapped into our
bowls, cleaned for the purpose with slices of bread, and
we set to with only a little less gusto.

The pudding, like the venison, was rich, almost too rich
for orphanage palates, but it was Christmas, and we
wouldn't taste plum pudding again till next year. So we
champed our way through it, hoping, yet dreading, to find
a threepenny bit, because to choke to death on a threepenny was a punishable offence; and then we sat back,
rather stodgily, with mugs of water poised for the Christmas toasts.

These toasts, in spite of the water, were seldom drunk.
What happened was that the Warden stood up and pro-
posed a toast to someone or other, and we cheered, at first
moderately, and then with rising hysteria. The matrons,
housemasters and teachers were cheered with dutiful affection, the benefactors were cheered dubiously, remembering
the venison. Then we worked through 'Old Boys and Girls',
'The Orphanage', 'The Founder' (we all craned round
and stared at the shadowy portrait over the door), 'Absent
Friends', 'Our Guests', and, finally, 'Ourselves'. After this

some quaking child would pipe 'The Warden!' and by
this time we were so worked up that the tablecloths were
dragged off and waved like flags, and the mugs pounded
on the bare tables. The Warden went off to dress as Santa
Claus and scare the daylights out of the nursery children,
and we were sent, penitentially, to wash the dishes.

The afternoon dragged on in a surfeit of Snakes and
Ladders. For some reason orphans are supposed to be par-
tial to this game, and we always received huge stocks of
them at Christmas time. Outside it was cold and grey, inside it was stuffy. We shook dice and moved counters and
yawned, and Matron said we needed a good long walk to
work off all that dinner; but, having done very well herself, no doubt, in the staff dining room, she made no move
to carry out her threat, and so we mooned over the garish
boards and the green serpents till the first gong rang for
tea.

The tea consisted of bread and syrup, which none of
us could face, but there were crackers and paper hats, and
we could make as much noise as we wanted. This fresh
surge of festivity seemed to freshen us all up, so that by
the time we finished we were in fine fettle for the dance
at seven o'clock.

I shall never forget those orphanage dances! Once again
we trekked up to the West Block, in our Sunday dresses,
and with our boots newly polished. The hall had been
cleared, the forms and tables piled round the walls, and
the gas globes sent long shining paths over the floor, where
the housemasters were scattering a reckless tin of Slipper-
ine. As we took off our coats and keeked into little bits of
mirror the boys arrived, blustering and swaggering, with
their Sunday chokers, and a fair sprinkling of kilts. The
working girls, living a perplexing semi-adult life in domestic training, came in last of all, in white blouses and striped
ties, with their long hair in magnificent ribbons. At any
minute the dance would start.

In came the Headmaster, Mr. Robinson, tall, silver-haired, bowing gracefully to the cheers as he made his way to the piano. In came the Warden, to even louder cheers. *He* was carrying a violin. The strings were plucked and tightened, a dance was announced, and away we went, boots, chokers and all, scraping and slithering to all the tunes of the day. 'Bye, Bye Blackbird' was our standard foxtrot, 'Blaze Away' our quickstep, and we had quite a selection of waltzes of the one-two-three, one-two-three style.

Sometimes a boy would march up to a matron, in tongue-tied gallantry, and butt her desperately through the throng. Sometimes the Warden would lay aside his violin, select a girl, and support her, blushing and drooping, on to the floor. We all danced except the Treasurer, who sat in a corner and did crosswords; and the Warden's fiddle bow dominated the evening. Blindfolded, he used it to point out the winning couple in spot dances; he stirred and prodded on the couples who were inclined to moon about and hold up the traffic; and on one awful occasion when etiquette was infringed by a girl not only refusing to dance with a partner, but knocking him down and jumping on him, the bow paused in 'The Merry Widow' to do duty as a cane.

At half-time the younger children were buttoned into their coats and sent home, and the seniors, glad of the elbow room, were served with slabs of Christmas cake, a heavy, sustaining sort of delicacy which only an orphan could digest. During this interval the Headmaster played softly, and introduced us to the tunes of the outside world: 'Wheeziana', 'When it's Springtime in the Rockies', and 'River, stay 'way from my Door'. We leaned against the piano, quietly happy. Some time we would be leaving the orphanage, a year, two years, and we would be free to wear what we liked, and do whatever we wanted. And yet . . . there was a magic about the present too, an inarticulate joy which was bound up with the gaslight and the music and the hundreds of faces round us. The warning stood out in the

great stone fireplaces, REMEMBER THY CREATOR IN THE DAYS
OF THY YOUTH, and our youth was a happy time. We were
happier now than when we were cheering our heads off at
dinnertime, but because such moments of ecstasy can be
too intense to last long, we were almost relieved to hear
the Warden say, 'Take your partners for a Paul Jones!'
and to know that once more we were ready for the fray.

We went home at ten o'clock, muffled up against the
sharp frost, and yawning. Some of us would be sick that
night. Matron said so, and Matron was usually right. But it
had been a wonderful Christmas, our stockings filled, the
sausages, the stew, the crackers, the dance . . . and it wasn't
over yet.

There was still the carol service, when choir-boys would
sing solos, and the tiniest children would be allowed up
to sing 'Away in a Manger'. Next week it would be New
Year, with another dance, this time till midnight, and with
hot tea served with the leaden cake. Someone would wire
a radio up to a speaker—we considered this a major elec-
tronic feat—and at twelve o'clock we would stand hushed
to hear the solemn tones of Big Ben reverberate through
the hall; then the Warden would shout 'A Happy New
Year, everybody!' and we would yell back, our ears and
throats splitting, *The same to you, sir!*' and someone
would grab the dinner bells and clang them till they were
grabbed and taken from him.

After that, Christmas would really be past for another
year. The new annuals would be dog-eared and shabby,
the Christmas toys would be broken, the dice and tiddley-
winks scattered. We would have had our school party, the
Guide party in the village, and the party for the children who
didn't qualify for any of the other parties; and by that time
the neglected children, the unwanted and unlucky ones
who hadn't had presents, would be called to the study
and consoled with sympathy and good wishes and yet another set of Snakes and Ladders.

5

Promotion

W HEN I was twelve, I was moved up from the Rectory to the Big Dayroom. Now I was a 'big quean'. I got an extra half-slice of bread and an extra biscuit for tea, and I could no longer avoid domestic duties. A rota was pinned up on the dayroom wall, and there was our round of work, planned out for weeks ahead. There was an almost military emphasis on doing things properly. Thus, when cleaning the dormitories, we never swept *under* the beds. We lifted them out, swept behind them, and lifted—not pulled—them back. Caster alignment was as strict as in any hospital, and when we polished the endowment plates on the walls, with their Olde Englishe lettering, heaven help us if we left a speck of metal polish on a benefactor's name !

Washing up was done on an assembly-line system, drying each item twice, and leaving the cloths, sink and floor spotless. On Saturdays we cleaned the cutlery, and every single fork was inspected. We did it the hard way, with powdered bathbrick. We did everything the hard way. We had to grate down the bathbrick ourselves, rub lumps of carbolic soap on our scrubbers, and even mix up our own blacking from filthy little packets of stuff like treacly tar.

My new matron, Miss Nicholson, took no more kindly to my lack of domesticity than the Wife had done. Incidentally, the nickname 'the Wife' was out in the Big Dayroom. To refer thus to Miss Rae was to stamp oneself as a 'booby' just out of the Rectory. Big queans called her 'Susie', and soon I began to feel that Susie's opinion of me was higher than Miss Nicholson's.

Most of the girls liked Miss Nicholson, who was newer to
the orphanage than me. She had been in India, I remember, and had heavily bandaged legs, which must have
troubled her a lot on our long walks. So far as I can recall, I
think she was kind, but she never took to me. There was
something about me that rubbed her up the wrong way.
Whereas Susie would yell at me and then turn away to
hide a smile, Miss Nicholson froze me with disapproval;
and I never knew why.

I never got the chance to find out. One day she was
cutting our hair in the bathroom, and singeing the ends
with a candle—a sophisticated, and to us exotic operation
—when she cried suddenly, 'Oh! Oh, my head!' and went
out. We never saw her again. Nurse went to her room when
she didn't appear for supper, and found her unconscious.
The doctor came, an ambulance arrived, and she was taken
to the Fleming Hospital with meningitis. For two days the
Warden himself took morning prayers, and explained to us
that things were very grave, and that we could only hope,
and pray for her; and on the third day he announced to us
that she had died.

This was drama of the first importance. Half of the girls
gave themselves up to an orgy of grief, wandering about
inarticulate with sobs, their faces swollen, their eyes glazed.
In a frenzy of self-sacrifice we offered up our pocket money
to buy a wreath, and at the graveside the reverent jostling
to see just where our wreath would go was a great help in
distracting attention from the last dreadful moments.

Next day we were told that one of our late matron's
relations had been so touched by our gesture that he had
left a sum of money to be divided among us, and on the
next pocket-money day we would all get threepence extra.
We came out of our mourning with a jerk, and after that,
when any of the staff looked off-colour, we speculated
ghoulishly on how much we would make if the worst came
to the worst.

The author and her twin brother, aged eight, before they went to Aberlour Orphanage

Dorothy and Leonard, aged twelve, at the time of the author's Plea. This was taken on a day trip to Inverness

Children in lines in the school playground, 1926. The boys' hair
has the regulation crop

Entrance Hall, East Block. The 'sacred front entrance' used only
by visitors

A group of working girls. 'Living a perplexing semi-adult life . . . they had what to us seemed dizzy privileges'

Boys from the Mitchell Wing of the orphanage. The author's future husband circled

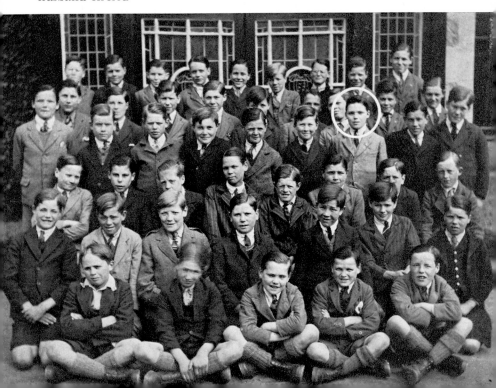

Clan Dormitory, Mitchell Wing, West Block. Each bed was dedicated to a different clan, and wore its tartan

Dining Hall, East Block. "We were demons for thick bread"

The original orphanage building. The orphanage was founded by
Canon Charles Jupp in 1875

East Block before the fire. This is where the author lived

West Block. The boys' end, containing the McCorquodale hall and the Warden's study

West Block rebuilt after the fire. The gardens never regained their former glory

Dean Wolfe with the author, 1960, on a visit to her home in Lanark

Dean Wolfe and Spey, with the orphanage in the background, around 1957

Dean Wolfe talks to the author while Eamonn Andrews and Mrs. Wolfe listen

This is Your Life

Aberlour Orphanage choir with Dean and Mrs. Wolfe in the centre; Rev. Michael Wolfe and the author are on the left at the back

During my stay at the orphanage, from 1929 to 1933, matrons were paid about a pound a week and all found, which, though adequate enough in the thirties, was small recompense for all they had to do. They were on the go from half past six in the morning till after eight at night, and even then they were on call. When well on in their sixties they tramped the roads and the moors with us, and kept us under control. While we were at school they patched sheets and sliced bread and did a host of other little jobs, and in the evenings they cut hair and supervised homework or bathing or the mending of our clothes. We were responsible for our own mending, and, furthermore, every child was numbered, chronologically, and this number had to be embroidered, laboriously, in chain stitch, on every single garment. Mine was 3659, which shows how many children had passed through the orphanage since it was founded in 1875.

Matrons got two hours off one week, and a 'long day' from ten in the morning till ten at night every other week. Wisely, they got off the premises in their free time. Usually they went to Elgin, where we imagined them drifting in and out of cinemas and cafés and buying boxes of chocolates and even smoking cigarettes. In actual fact, I think they saved most of their money for their summer holidays, when the younger ones came back with their hair permed and a supply of new, fashionable clothes.

The older matrons never seemed to buy anything new at all. There were two sisters, Miss Mary and Miss Lizzie Davidson, who had charge of the youngest girls and the youngest boys, and who had come to the orphanage as young women. When I knew them they were small, elderly ladies who wore ageless clothes with fancy flowered hats on Sundays. Miss Lizzie, the younger one, was always very perjink, with grey marcelled hair and a walking stick. Miss Mary's hair was scraped back in a bun, and she scurried about, stooping, with the beginnings of a hump on her back.

c

She spent all her money on her children. When they coughed in the night she got up and soothed them with unofficial honey and lemon drinks. She bought them hair ribbons, too, for Sunday. 'Little girls like to look nice,' she said, putting on her old navy-blue coat for yet another season. 'The bairns get little enough.'

Miss Lizzie was just as devoted to her boys. She organised dances and singsongs for them on wet days, and her last words every evening were, 'Good night, my chickens!' 'Good night, mother hen!' the children would shout back. Her charges never forgot her. Once I saw her being photographed between two of her 'laddies', now men six feet tall. The photographer found it difficult to get the three heads into the picture. 'Right!' said the men, and lifted the little old lady by the elbows. 'Put me *down*!' she demanded, her feet kicking helplessly. 'I've seen the time I'd have skelped your bottoms for that!'

'Just try it!' the men taunted her; and they kept her there, fuming, till she gave them each a kiss.

Living on top of us all the time, the matrons must have been glad of the chance to get away on their own. They dined and sat together in the matrons' sitting room, and for privacy each had her own quarters, a room so tiny that they were never tempted to escape to it for long. These small rooms intrigued us. We were never allowed inside, and matrons seemed to slide in and out, drawing the door behind them, so that we never got more than a glimpse of the luxuries we believed they possessed.

To us, the furnishings *were* luxurious, the little bit of carpet on the floor, the chintz curtains, the reflection, in the dressing-table mirror, of a quilt on the bed. Sometimes, too, we smelt perfume and powder which excited us greatly.

We, in the meantime, had no matron at all. We were left in charge of whoever had time to see to us, and most often that was the Under-Housekeeper. In my time there was a succession of people in this post, a job I wouldn't have had for the world. It wasn't only that the unfortunate person was chivvied about to any place where she was needed. The main trouble was that she was directly subordinate to Miss McKee, and subordinate was the operative word.

Miss McKee was Irish, straight mouth, straight back, and the strictest and most unbending person in the orphanage. She never settled for anything less than perfection. The maids that she trained stayed trained for life. I used to think she had no weaknesses at all, till one day, in a wee shop in the village, I surprised her gulping down a furtive saucer of ice-cream. She gave me a guilty but warning smile, and with a mental genuflection I withdrew, and told no one.

About twenty years after this, when she had retired, I met her by arrangement in Elgin, and remembering this incident, decided to take some ice-cream home for tea. Miss McKee insisted on paying. I said no, it had been my idea. We argued politely, back and forward, till at last she said, in that steely tone I remembered so well, '*I'll* get the ice-cream, Dorothy!'

At once I was ten years old again. 'Yes, Miss McKee,' I murmured.

One such personality would have been enough, but, to complicate things, Miss McKee was an identical twin, and sometimes her sister, a hospital matron from Leith, came to stay with her. Invariably we got them mixed up, as we indulged in rash confidences. 'We like you better than your sister, Miss McKee. Miss McKee's an old hag. But you won't tell Miss McKee, will you, Miss McKee? Couldn't you change jobs with Miss McKee and be *our* Miss McKee, Miss McKee?'

'But I *am* your Miss McKee,' she would say, with an edge in her voice that should have convinced us.

'Oh no you're not! Our Miss McKee's not as nice as you. Our Miss McKee gives us the belt!' We would pour

out these frank and defamatory statements till at last it
dawned on us that the person listening *was*, regrettably,
'our' Miss McKee, and later on her sister wondered why the
girls didn't come and talk to her any more.

However, Miss McKee knew perfectly well what she
was doing. Her training stuck to us, and of all the girls who
trembled under her rule there were few who could not
remember some kindness she had shown. There was one
tough and inarticulate child who used to slip in every night
for a quick kiss. The child told no one, and it wasn't till
many years later that Miss McKee told me. She must have
had many secrets like that.

I asked her once what kind of a child I had been when
I was under her care. She looked me straight in the eye
and told me. 'You were the biggest chatterbox I ever met.
You never once stopped talking. . . .'

Well, I asked for it.

As well as moving up to the Big Dayroom, I had now passed
my Qualifying Exam and was in the Advanced Division.
This gave a delightful variety to our schooldays. Not only
did we have different teachers for different subjects, but
some of the teachers were *men*. The one we all set our caps
at was Tommy Robertson, the maths teacher, blue-eyed,
curly-haired, with plus-fours and a farmer's stride. He
was, in fact, a farmer at Wester Elchies, across the Spey
(we could see his house from our window), and he turned
up romantically at nine every morning in a sports car,
and with a college scarf wound round his neck.

As well as the usual school subjects, the boys did woodwork and farming (with a view to future employment) and
the girls were given a course in domestic science. At this time
we had no woodwork or cookery room, so once a week we
were marched off to the village school for special instruc-
tion. It was not altogether a happy arrangement. Our class,
at least, got off to a bad start on the very first lesson.

We were to make Brown George Puddings, small gingery steamed puddings in individual basins. As the orphanage supplied the ingredients, the completed food was sent back, to be disposed of according to its palatability. Miss McKee had the first choice. If she felt that it was less than *cordon bleu*, she passed it on to the matrons, or, failing that, the laundry maids, or, in the last resort, the working girls. Any frank failures were tactfully removed at source.

There were twenty-four pupils in the class, and twenty-three passable puddings. The twenty-fourth stuck to the basin and broke when it was turned out. 'All right,' said the teacher laconically, 'just eat that one.' She had no idea what she was starting.

In a second the tiny pudding vanished under a scrum of twenty-four desperate pupils. Whether anyone actually got a piece I don't know. It took some time for us to sort ourselves out, and then we stood at our tables, humiliated and shamed, as the teacher lectured us.

'. . . never seen anything like it in my life! *Wild animals* wouldn't behave like that. Sheer and absolute greed . . .!'

True, of course. But . . . well, a little understanding of the circumstances would have made such a difference. It wasn't that we were hungry, apart from the normal healthy hunger around dinnertime. It was just that we had the chance, for once, to taste something different.

I never really enjoyed my cookery lessons at the village school. Of course, I was not an ideal pupil. I talked too much, and wouldn't concentrate on the job. Once, when we were watching someone trying to turn pancakes on a girdle, I was rash enough to snigger at her clumsiness. In a flash Miss Smith turned on me.

'Right. *You* do it.'

She pushed the knife into my right hand. I changed it to my left, and her lips tightened. Now, a left-handed person may *look* awkward, but isn't necessarily awkward at all. I

could see, however, that I was expected to make a mess of
things, and that is just what happened. I flipped the pan-
cake right off the stove, and made matters worse with a
sharp giggle. Miss Smith shook her head, and obviously
wanted to shake me as well. 'I thought so !' she said. 'Handless. Utterly handless !'

It looked as if Miss Rae was going to be right. I would
never make a worker !

One morning we were told that a new matron had been
engaged for us, and was to arrive next day.

I think we were all relieved. For some time we had been
getting out of hand. We'd had more freedom than usual,
but somehow we didn't enjoy it. This matron, we were
told, was young. Furthermore, she was a Guide Captain,
so we would no longer have to depend on the services of
volunteer Guiders from the village. We would have someone of our very own.

Miss Gray caused quite a sensation when she arrived,
wearing a kilt, and a blazer with a Dundee Ladies' Hockey
Club badge. Right away, she scored a success by showing
us how to set our hair in a way which would not offend
Miss McKee's sensibilities. (Miss McKee had quite a
Brocklehurstian attitude to coiffeurs.) She promised to teach
us hockey and netball, and she took us walks beyond the
scope of our former more elderly matrons.

But it was as a Guide Captain that she made her mark.

We were all lounging about the hall on our meeting
night, indifferently dressed, when the door opened, and
in came Miss Gray, immaculate, full uniform, white shirt,
all round cords, the lot. Briskly, she halted, and gave us a
full salute. We drew ourselves up, somewhat shaken. After
a second, heels clicked, hands raised to hats, in a silence of
admiration and pride. Not a word was said, but from now
on, we felt, the 2nd Aberlour company was going to go up
in the world.

6

Snake in the Grass

It must have been about this time that I was confirmed.

Every winter a block of children of suitable age were detailed for Confirmation classes. We rather looked forward to the ceremony. It was a break with routine, and it gave us a chance to be upsides with our seniors who went once a month for Holy Communion. It was not that we particularly relished the idea of getting up early to go to church; it was merely that we thought we might be missing something.

Nor were we too enthusiastic about the prospect of 'classes'. We were told that we would have to take notes, and that later on there would be a sort of exam to see if we had taken in all that we needed to know, because if we didn't understand what it was all about there was no point in being 'done'. I know there is great clerical disapproval of that phrase, but that is how we looked on it, I'm afraid: an initiation rather than a spiritual experience.

On a Wednesday evening, therefore, with our boots polished, our hair combed, and with clean pinafores on, we lined up in the passage, kicking our heels with boredom. As usual, Wolfie was late. We waited half an hour before Spey came prancing along to tell us all was well, and then Wolfie bustled up, opened the glass door to the sacred front entrance, and led us into the study.

We had never been in this room before, and now we let out a great sigh of ecstasy. The curtains were drawn, the carpet was soft and thick, and the polished furniture glowed in the firelight. It was so cosy that we groaned, 'Oh, *sir*!' when Wolfie went to light the gas, so he laughed and agreed to leave things as they were.

I suppose that on subsequent occasions we must have had more light, because we went through the Creed and the Catechism in some depth, and took notes for the forthcoming written test; but my main memory of Confirmation classes is of a group of us sitting on a rug at the Warden's feet, with the fire flickering red on the walls, and sweets being passed round, and eventually being chased out because we had talked so long and listened so ardently that it was well past our bedtime.

Sometimes Mr. Corke, the Subwarden with the sledge, took the classes instead, and led us into all sorts of arguments and suppositions. One fascinating theory which he passed on to us had a queerly sickening effect on me, and still haunts me on Good Friday services. 'Christ died, not as a result of crucifixion alone, but of a broken heart. After his death, when the soldiers pierced his side, water and blood gushed out; and it is a medical fact that when a person's heart is ruptured, water mingles with the blood . . .' This was offered, not as a dogma, but as interesting information.

Every Sunday we were prayed for in church, and there was always some wit to whisper along the pews, as we knelt smirking, 'Let us pray for the Confirmation Candy Dates. . . .'

As the time drew nearer (the classes seemed to go on interminably) we became more and more excited. We were briefed on the ceremony, and, what was of more consequence, were fitted out for the occasion. I had hoped, somehow, that we would be garbed in white, with something like a bridal veil, but the orphanage did not run to white dresses, so we had to fall back on navy blue. Every available navy dress was mustered, till everybody managed to find one to fit. On the day of the service the chattering but nervous candidates put on these rough navy frocks, and then reported to Miss McKee to be 'trimmed up'. White collars and cuffs were pinned on, with pricks and jags inflicted on both sides, and then came the veil; not the bride-like gossamer I had hoped for, but a square of what was probably starched cotton, with an embroidered cross in front.

In itself this veil was quite attractive; in theory the whole outfit was neat and smart; but Miss McKee insisted that veils should be tight over the brows, with no hair showing. There were girls whose looks survived this handicap fairly well, but I wore glasses, and school glasses, at that time, were steel-rimmed and unflattering. I began to inch my veil upwards, but Miss McKee glared at me and told me to leave it alone. So there I was, with my veil too tight, and my feet in heavy boots and long black stockings, so acutely dissatisfied with my appearance that I was in no condition to go to church, let alone be confirmed.

However, I was not the only one with problems. Lined up in the dayroom, ready to move off, we were all suddenly smitten with the desire to run to the lavatory. 'Right,' said Miss Gray. 'Off you go, the lot of you, and don't be long.' We lined up again, and were just at the front door when Jeannie, a somewhat hysterical child whose nerves always affected her in the same way, put up her hand. 'Please, ma'am, I need to . . .'

'But you've just been.'

'I know, but . . .'

Another pause, as Jeannie dashed away, and then we were out in the sunshine, two by two, walking sedately, along the drive, into the churchyard, over the rustic bridges . . .

Just at the church door, Jeannie wavered again.

'Please, ma'am, I need to . . .'

'Oh, go on with you!' said Matron desperately. 'It's too late now!'

Once in the church, Jeannie managed to restrain herself fairly well, and I had time to worry about Lilian. Lilian was seated beside me, with her foot on a large hassock. She had fluid on the knee, and for the past week had been in bed, but she had been allowed up on condition that she did not kneel. Now she nudged me and told me that she'd be too embarrassed to be confirmed standing. If she knelt, would I, as the candidate coming after her, help her to her feet?

'Don't be silly,' I said. 'You were told to stand.'

'But the Bishop won't get his hands on my head.'

'Well, *he* can stand.'

We went off into smothered giggles, and Jeannie, next to Lilian, wriggled desperately and begged us not to make her laugh. 'Ssh-ssh!' said Matron, glaring along the row, and we all stood up as the procession entered from the vestry, beginning with Spey, and ending with the Bishop of Moray.

It was the longest service I ever remember. We sat through the long hot afternoon as Bishop Mclean addressed us, benignly but endlessly, and the crammed pews were in a general fidget before he finished. Our navy frocks itched like hair shirts, the pins on our collars pricked, and our veils made us sweat. Then the actual Confirmation began, boys first. We scanned their faces as they went back to their seats, wondering if they might have changed, whether they would be mitred with flames, or suddenly eloquent in mysterious tongues . . . but no. They were a little redder in the face, perhaps, but swaggeringly unconcerned.

Our turn now. Pew by pew. The Bishop droned on, tired old hands on so many heads, the great ring flashing on his finger. 'Defend O Lord this thy child with thy Heavenly Grace . . .'

I had no chance to ponder on higher things. Jeannie had been kept waiting so long that she was now in desperation. Unable to stand still, she began to whirl round and

round like a dervish, till suddenly she found herself at the
Bishop's feet. For a few tense moments she was still. The
laying-on of hands was accomplished. 'The Lord be with
you,' said the Bishop. Primly, correctly, Jeannie replied,
'And with thy spirit,' and then went sprinting down the
aisle and out of the door before anyone realised she had gone.

Lilian next, limping forward with her bandaged knee.
'Don't kneel,' whispered Wolfie, but, gallantly, Lilian knelt.
All went well till she found she couldn't rise. Wolfie step-
ped forward to take one arm, I went to take the other, but
Lilian was nothing if not independent. Planting both elbows
on the Bishop's lap, she heaved herself to her feet, while
the Bishop jerked galvanically with the shock. 'Dorothy
Kate,' I heard the Warden announcing. It was my turn
next. . . .

But if the Confirmation service was disappointing, our
first Holy Communion made up for it. We were to go
to the 7 a.m. service on the first Sunday in May, and this
happened to be the weekend when my father was up
visiting us, so that he was able to come along too. It was
one of those perfect mornings which seem lovelier in Aberlour than anywhere else, the sun bright gold, the leaves
green and newly fledged, and all the stained-glass windows
glowing. Even in the church the song of the birds was a
choir in itself, but here, at this hour, there was no choir,
only the soft voice of the priest and the acolytes moving
silently in scarlet cassocks. We tiptoed up and knelt as we
had been shown, hands crossed, heads bowed, and it was
no irreverence at all to squint up through our lowered
lashes and catch the solemn glance of a large Labrador
curled on the altar steps as his master went from hand to
hand with the silver chalice.

'Did you like it?' we asked our father, as we walked
home after the service. 'Did you enjoy it?'

He was very moved by the experience. As the only
non-Episcopal member of the family (he was an elder in

the Church of Scotland) he had not taken Communion with us, but Wolfie had approached him earlier and told him he could do so if he wished. He refused, feeling that he was not familiar enough with the service, but the offer had been made, and was very much appreciated.

There were some girls, older than me, who had not been confirmed, and whose confirmation had been deferred indefinitely. These were the unfortunate ones who mentally or educationally were not quite up to the mark; the children who were always behind, dragging along with all sorts of handicaps which at that time had to be endured rather than alleviated.

At first, these children had shocked me. I was sorry for them, but I didn't want to associate with them. I kept myself aloof from the bed-wetters, forever washing and drying their soiled sheets, and the girls whose heads were shaven because of ringworm. Suppose *I* were to catch it and have my head shaved?

It didn't take long, however, to learn to accept all the tragedies and oddities, and to look on them as a normal part of life. I even learned to enjoy their stories, in a macabre sort of way. Eva, who was next in age to me, used to toss off her tale casually, but with great effect.

'I went into the coal cellar, and the door wouldn't open. It was my father. He was hanging from the roof, and he had a rope round his neck, and a belt round his waist, and his stomach was all swollen. There was a big hole in his throat, and the blood was all over his shirt. . . .'

'What did you do?' we asked breathlessly.

'I went for my mother, but she was ill. She was dying. Then a man came and cut him down. His face was all black, and his tongue was sticking out.'

Not a tear, not a shudder. She stuck her tongue out to the root, squinted horribly, and held her breath, and we egged her on, eager for more.

'And what happened then?'

'Oh, the police came. Then the Salvation Army came, and took us away, and one of them brought us here.'

Superficially, one would have said that this experience had made no mark on her. She was impish and mischievous, and bereavement had not affected her appetite; but she kept on telling her story, again and again. She couldn't stop talking about it, and Miss Gray, sitting nearby, made no move to stop her. She made no comment at all, even when Eva singled her out, and, rather boastfully, told the story once more, neither embellished nor diminished. In time, she talked it out of her system.

Joan Morris preferred not to talk about her traumatic experience. She was a refined, intelligent, but delicate girl, the only one I knew who admitted to living 'up a close'. (I lived up one too, but though I didn't deny it, I alluded to it discreetly. Our room and kitchen became 'an upper-storey flat'.)

Joan's father drank too much, worked seldom, and bullied his wife. One day he demanded money when there was none, and Mrs. Morris, at the end of her tether, drank lysol. Joan came home in time to hear her screaming, and screamed herself because the neighbours wouldn't let her go in. She wrote home once a month, urging her father to turn over a new leaf. He never replied.

Then there was Lily Green, who had been abandoned on a doorstep and brought up in Aberlour. Lily always insisted that she had a mother who one day would come to to take her home. The mother did turn up when Lily was fourteen, and old enough to earn money. The orphanage, knowing her mother's occupation, advised Lily against going to the woman who, up till now, had shown no interest, and they found her a job sufficiently far away to make visiting difficult; but soon rumours began to circulate that Lily had met up with her mother, and was following the same profession.

Sometimes children came to Aberlour from other orphanages. One day we came home from school to see a beautiful blonde head at the dayroom window. When the head turned round we saw that what had been a pretty face was terribly mangled, her mouth twisted sideways, a dreadful dimple above one ear, and one of her hands helpless. 'I fell three storeys high,' she greeted us.

We had our share of cripples, club feet, calipers, the results of untreated birth injuries, polio, accidents or just ill-treatment. They quickly fell into the orphanage routine; they even went barefoot, which was supposed to be beneficial, and they kept up remarkably well on walks. The big worry was what was to become of them when it was time to earn their own living.

Fortunately, the orphanage did not entirely cast its charges off. Any child was welcome to come back, at any time, and quite often there would be a cross-section of old boys and girls taking advantage of this hospitality, some of them smart, successful, and inclined to show off a little, others homesick for the only home they had known, and a few rogues and layabouts lying low till the Warden kitted them out, fed them, found them a job and sent them on their way.

Most of them, in time, seemed to find some niche or other. But there were always the few who dragged along, several classes behind the others, inadequate and unwanted. They found it difficult to obey orders quickly, the smarter girls bullied them, and when they rebelled, in sudden wild flashes of temper (somebody was once pushed gloriously into the bathing pond), *they* were the ones who attracted attention and got themselves into trouble.

It was so easy to take advantage of them; and now, well settled in, gaining a certain amount of influence as I grew older, I shocked myself one day by realising that contact with these poor souls was making me callous. At one time I could have wept for them when they were teased.

Now I found that I was capable of being cruel to them myself.

The revelation took place one pocket-money day. I had my threepence a week to spend as against the normal penny, and this affluence meant that I could show off with expensive sweets like chocolate and marshmallows while the others went in for more economical and longer-lasting stuff. Most of the time, however, I shopped as carefully as anyone else. I liked to get the benefit of my money.

Cathie Brown was one of the girls who seldom got her full quota of cash, because she was for ever in debt for little errors like not having her boots polished, or appearing at table with dirty hands, and so on. She was the kind of child who nowadays would be sent to a special school. She had a crooked faced and sad eyes, like a child in a Mervyn Peake drawing, and she had been born with a cleft palate, which affected her speech. We could understand her, in a rough sort of way, but strangers and impatient people couldn't make head or tail of what she was saying, and she was classed as being more stupid than she really was.

On the occasion which has pricked my conscience for so long, a group of us had set off to spend our pocket money as soon as school was over. It was late October, frosty, and already dusk. The shops had their gases lit, and we ran wild and free in the long quiet street, from Miss Thirde's, cheery, plump Miss Thirde with the whitewashed shop with toffee apples on the counter and aprons and shampoos strung above, to Walker the baker's, who sold bags of broken biscuits (and who was courting our Qualifying teacher); to the newsagent's with the slot machines for chewing gum, which we weren't supposed to buy, to the sprawling shop at the end of the street, where things were always cheaper, but more fusty, as if they had been mixed up with the firelighters. There were two shops in the square, one of them the little shop where in summer

Miss McKee ate her ice-cream in a saucer, in a stone
kitchen at the back; and when all these were exhausted,
and if we didn't feel like a bag of brown sugar at Kelman
the grocer's, there was a little shop down a side lane, a dark
little shop we always left till last.

Tonight, in honour of Guy Fawkes, there were a few
Bengal matches and an odd sparkler littered about the
window, but these created no stir. Our twelve-year-old
appetites craved for sweets. And then, in a corner, we saw
a box of small conical objects, about an inch high,
labelled 'Snake in the Grass'.

'What'll those be?' somebody asked.

'Dunno. Sherbet, maybe.'

'What? A ha'penny for that? *I'm* not buying it!'

'I'd like to know what they are. . . .'

'They're only a ha'penny.' They were looking at me,
the one with the extra money, the one who could afford
to take a risk. But I shook my head. I wanted treacle toffee.

Then along the pavement came a group of smaller girls,
waiting for us to move along, and let them have a look.
Cathie Brown was there. Her long face was pale in the
gaslight, and queer guttural gruntings came from her
crooked mouth. We watched them all, tolerantly, from our
side of the window. What a row kids made!

They, too, had spotted the Snake in the Grass. They,
too, were curious, but none of them had any money left;
no one but Cathie, who had a ha'penny, for once, and she
had a passion for liquorice comfits.

It was then that I got my idea. Cathie would do anything I asked. She got no advantage from this, but I knew
that I could coax her to oblige me.

'Hey, Cathie,' I said, treacherously matey, 'how about
buying that Snake in the Grass?'

She stared at me for a long time, considering. 'What is
it?' she said at last. We knew what she was saying, but
nobody else would have understood.

'That's what we want to find out,' I said patiently.

Another pause. She scanned the box dubiously, and shook her head. Cathie could be stubborn sometimes.

'Go on, Cathie. See what it is. We're all dying to know.'

She didn't want to. We could all see that, but she was outnumbered, one of the kind who will always be outnumbered. Reluctantly, she made for the door of the shop, and we all trooped in after her, to explain what she wanted.

It was a fascinating shop to go into. There was a frosted-glass door, a red papered passage and a steep flight of carpeted stairs. Down these stairs would come an old Victorian-looking lady with a paraffin lamp in her hand. The whole place stank of paraffin, and on the wall of the passage, as the lamp drew nearer, you could see a framed set of verses, announcing that this was a Temperance House —I never got time to read to the last verse. We were always hustled into the dark shop, where the lamp was put down on the counter, and the woman waited, benevolently, while we made our choice.

This time we were met by a man in a greasy cap and a scarf round his throat. He didn't put the lamp down, he held it, and the flame jigged and made dreadful shadows on his face.

'What d'ye want?' he asked irritably. If it hadn't been for the poem in the passage we'd have sworn he smelt of beer.

Cathie began to stutter, and we all rushed to the rescue.

'She wants a Snake in the Grass.'

His fingers rattled in a box and picked one out. The ha'penny was handed over, and we all marched into the frosty night.

Cathie, in the midst of a sort of scrum, turned the Snake over and over in her hands. She wasn't happy about it. It's purpose was still obscure. Someone snatched it from her and passed it round, and by the time she got it back it was oozing white powder. Maybe it was sherbet? Cathie dipped in her pinkie, licked the edge, and said 'Eugh!' so we gathered it wasn't for eating.

There was only one thing to be done. We went back to the shop, and waited for the mufflered man to come back down with the lamp.

'What's this Snake in the Grass *for*, mister?'

Seeing the chance of trade and profit vanishing, he was less than civil.

'It's a firework,' he grumbled. 'You light it.'

'Oh!' We scuffled out for another conference, as the lamplight wavered unsteadily up the stairs. It took us some time to realise that we didn't have any matches. Nobody wanted to go back this time. Some thought that I, as the eldest and richest, should risk it, while others thought that he might take more pity on Cathie. At last we decided to go in together. Cathie, as the purchaser, would ask for a match, and I would translate; but as the lamp flowered at the stairhead once more, we lost our nerve and bolted. The enormity of bringing him down to ask for free matches was just too much. Eventually, we got two from a man who happened to be passing. 'You're not smoking, are you?' he asked severely, and we assured him we were not. When he had gone we gathered into a huddle and prepared to light the Snake.

The first match went out. The second caused a dim glow at the bottom of the cone. 'Put it *down*!' we yelled, visualising Cathie going up in a phosphorescent blaze, and she propped it hurriedly into a corner of the shop doorway.

We needn't have worried. There was a feeble green flare, and then it sputtered out. That was all. Truculently, we stared at each other, not knowing whether to blame Cathie, the girl with the matches, or the manufacturer. At last we hit on the victim. The man with the muffler was responsible. I said so loudly, and everybody, baulked of the expected spectacle, backed me up.

The trouble with being an agitator is that you have to live up to your principles. Once more I put my hand on the knob of the frosted-glass door. Once more the smoky orange light appeared, and the truculent gentleman came down, breathing even more beerily. This time, however, I had loud and voluble support. We entered the shop. I took a deep breath, and launched into my complaint.

'This Snake in the Grass—it doesn't work.'

The man scowled, and mumbled his instructions again. 'It's a firework. You light it.'

Cathie began a solo and incomprehensible explanation of her own. The man stared at her, half frightened, as if she were some sort of foreigner, and I hastily shouted her down.

'It just sort of fizzled and went out. It was nothing. It's a swindle.'

'God Almighty!' said the shopkeeper, 'what do you *expect* for a ha'penny?'

It was the wrong question. We all knew exactly what a ha'penny was worth, and we proceeded to tell him. I think he was rather taken aback by all this, because when somebody said, 'And why's it called a Snake in the Grass, anyway?' he answered humbly enough, 'You light it and you see the Snake. It's green, intit? Well, then. The Snake's in the Grass.' We didn't get it. There were savage murmurs about getting our money back. The surly man looked us over, and decided to be fair.

'Look,' he said, picking another cone from the box, 'I'll light this.' He put a match to the blue paper, and laid it on the stone floor. There was another brief green flare, and he began to dance about and point eagerly with a dirty finger. 'There it is, see? See the Snake? See it?'

We didn't. The flare had been too short, and now we felt bewildered as well as cheated. The man had, presumably, made amends, but where did that get us? We were no better off, and yet . . .

'It's a swindle,' I heard myself saying. 'It's not worth a ha'penny. It's a shame taking money like that from a kid that can't speak properly . . .'

'It was all she had. She should get it back.'

The man at the counter suddenly lost his temper. 'Get out!' he roared, brandishing the lamp as if he would fling it at us. 'Get the hell out of here, and don't come back!'

We went crowding into the dim passage, and jostling at the door; and there we held a resentful post-mortem on the transaction. Cathie was nearly crying. This was her first pocket money for weeks, and she'd been looking forward to spending it. . . .

'Well, you spent it,' I pointed out, tartly. I was annoyed at the way things had turned out, and Cathie's blubbering was all I needed. Besides, everybody was looking at me as if I were to blame.

'Well, it wasn't my fault,' I went on. 'I couldn't help it if the blessed Snake was a dud. And, anyway, she's had two Snakes for the price of one. She wouldn't have had that if I hadn't complained.'

There was an uneasy muttering about threepence a week, and a hint that the least I could do was to make up to Cathie what she had lost. But I wasn't going to fall for that. I was fed up with the whole business. I ought to have known better than to get mixed up with kids in the first place. So I tossed my head and walked off with a last shot fired in bravado. 'Don't ask *me* to help you next time you get in a mess.'

I wish now that I had paid up. A ha'penny is all it would have cost me for peace of mind. Now nothing that I have can buy respite from the nagging guilt of all those years ago.

7

The end of an era

DURING our more disgruntled moments our greatest ambition was for the orphanage to burn down. We had discussed this endlessly in the dormitories, and we had our plans all worked out. We would feed the flames and sabotage the fire brigade (St. Trinian's had nothing on us) and then, free at last, we would hare off into the darkness. We always imagined it happening at night, roaring flames and trapped matrons and everyone else pouring down the drives like ants from a burning log.

When it did happen it was on a summer morning, and the fire got under way without any help from us.

June 13th, 1931; the superstitious thought that maybe the date had something to do with it. It was a perfect June day, and because it was a Saturday, we were busy with our extra domestic duties. Floors had been scrubbed, brasses polished, and cutlery cleaned, and we were all keeping out of Miss McKee's way because she was going to clear out the storeroom and wanted some volunteers.

For all the sunshine, it was dark indoors—too dark. A kind of fog hung about the passages, the pantry was hot and oppressive, and there was a smell of smoke in the kitchen. 'I canna understand it,' said Cook, looking at the clear fire in the range. 'Is somebody burning rubbish in the garden?'

'Look,' whispered a girl, peeping into the new-scrubbed dormitory. 'There's a red light behind the ventilators!'

'Come in here,' said Miss Gray, at the door of another dormitory. 'Don't you think it's awfully hot?'

I was no sooner in than the roof collapsed with a rumble. I stared, in utter surprise, at a counterpane bursting into flame under the red-hot debris, when Miss Gray yanked me backwards and dragged me clear. 'Get *out*, you fool!' she yelled.

From nowhere, three gardeners appeared, and began to drag out beds and hurl them down the steps. Bedroom number two was now on fire, and it seemed only moments till all the windows had forked flames curling out of them, and black smoke pouring up to the sky.

The Aberlour fire brigade arrived, three men and a hand-cart. The Dufftown, the Elgin and other fire engines came clanging up, more and more of them, from farther and farther away. Great pythons of hosepipe ran down the drive and over the lawns and right down to the river, and there was a most gratifying display of ladders, and firemen in helmets and gauntleted figures with axes. For one moment we were afraid that such a corps of experts would have the fire out before we had time to enjoy it; but soon we found that they were going to have a fight. This fire was serious.

Our own dayroom was impassable, but the Rectory, where the ten-year-olds lived, was being emptied ruthlessly. Beds, lockers, sheets, forms were flung out on to the lawn. Miss Rae saw her canary's cage heaved out of the window, and took a moment to pick it up and give it to someone to tend. A little huddle moved off, crooning, 'Poor wee Dickie. *Poor* wee Dickie!' to the small thing quivering on its perch.

Nigger was safe; he was yapping about, hindering everyone, and not taking kindly to being kissed because he'd had the sense not to be burned alive. Through the shattered front entrance the study was being cleared, shelves and shelves of books, ledgers with deckled edges, files and letters and cushions and portraits and pokers. People worked with a roar in their ears and the heat of the flames on their faces;

and how bizarre, how pathetic, was the debris of a home made derelict, a few toys and annuals side by side with a roll-top desk and a basket of darned stockings!

By this time the dining hall was blazing, every aperture sheeted in flame, the turrets roaring and whirling as they crashed, and the ivy shrivelled from the roofless walls. Everybody who had anything to do with the orphanage turned up to help—Tommy Robertson had seen the flames from his farm across the Spey, and had run all the way. As the small children were moved to safety at the West Block, the older boys came down to lend a hand. Somehow or other, our plans for a mass escape had been forgotten. Our home was on fire, and we had to do what we could; and anyway, it was more interesting here.

Luckily, there was no wind. Mercifully, there was no rain, and the salvage on the lawn lay in hot sunshine. Not a leaf of all the scattered papers moved, not a page fluttered. Old brown photographs stared at the sky, and Dickie moped in a little bower built by his anxious guardians.

Round at the back of the orphanage they were clearing the stores, though not quite as Miss McKee had intended. Sacks of meal and cereal were piled on the flower borders, and relays of us carried endless jars of jam to the West Block kitchen. My brother and I, glad to be together, moved what seemed to be mountains of soap and baskets of eggs. It was three o'clock before we were called to the West Block to eat, and then the soup had no salt, the pudding no sugar. We ate it without a murmur.

By evening we were dead beat and dirty, our pinafores solid with the spillage of the commodities we had carried. We had nothing to change into. Everything we possessed had gone, even our boots. The horrible red tammies would never be seen again, and on this count we felt that the orphanage had been sacrificed in a good cause. Strangely, we felt no regret. All we wanted was a hot bath and bed.

We couldn't have a bath—we had no towels—and though we had beds, the staff were still wondering where to put them. At last they got it all worked out. The big boys moved into tents in the playing fields, thrilled at the idea of camping out, and the younger ones crammed together to release a dormitory or two for the little girls We, the bigger ones, the 12–14-year-olds, had our beds packed into the school.

Tired as we were, we couldn't sleep. We were keyed up to screaming pitch. We kept up a constant run to the lavatories, we climbed to the windows to report on the fire still smouldering and flaring in corners, and we talked and giggled all night. Someone had found an old gramophone, and we cranked it up and played scratchy records over and over again. Once or twice our matron passed by in the corridor.

'Aren't you going to bed, please, ma'am?'

'Later on. Be quiet now, and try and get some sleep.'

We didn't know then that she had nowhere to go, and was wandering about till morning.

We slept eventually, and wakened very deflated. We felt stale and dirty, and the fire was no longer a splendid thing. Nevertheless, we managed breakfast, and at eleven o'clock lined up to go to church.

Mr. Corke took the service, because the Warden was on holiday in Bournemouth, as far away as he could possibly be. All yesterday, we had worried about Wolfie, what he would say, how he would feel. He had been recalled by telegram, and no doubt was even now on his way.

The church was full of sightseers, and they wept as we walked in, barefoot and shabby in our stained clothes. We tried to look smug and unconcerned as we sang hymns and listened to prayers of thanksgiving for our deliverance.

We had indeed been lucky. Not a child had been harmed. If the fire had happened at night, spreading so quickly, we wouldn't have had a chance. My father had had

more of a fright than we had. Someone had knocked at his
door at breakfast time with the Sunday paper screaming
'Big Orphanage Fire!' in thick black headlines. 'Here, Ted,
is this no' where your weans is?' And then, as he snatched
the paper, 'It's all right, there's naebody hurtit!'

But there were more ways than one of being hurt. During
the afternoon Miss Gray collapsed with sheer exhaustion,
and was carried off, her head lolling romantically on Mr.
Corke's shoulder, to be put to bed in somebody's room. It
began to rain, a grey, bitter rain, on the smouldering ruins
and still littered lawn; and suddenly, along by the
church, came the Warden, grave and tired after travelling
all night.

We stood silently, our hair draggled, our clothes damp.
We would not have dreamed of running to him at that
moment. He looked at the roofless walls, the sour drift of
smoke, the shattered glass and empty windows, and then,
in the rain, he took his hat off, and every one of us puckered
up our faces and cried. We weren't crying for the orphanage—or at least we thought we weren't. We were grieving
for him, because he shouldn't have come back to this. He
didn't deserve it.

There was no time for grief, though. The school had to be
used next morning, and the beds would have to go elsewhere.
Miraculously a marquee appeared, and was erected with
commendable speed in the playground. It was like sleeping
in a circus, and by this time we were ready for sleep. The
gramophone had vanished, and the last thing I remember
was Wolfie looking in to check that we were all right.

By Monday, the sleeping problem was still with us. The
marquee, I think, was only on loan, and anyway was not
suitable for permanent living. But where else were we to
go?

'Why not drain the bathing pond?' asked somebody.

'Wouldn't do,' said Wolfie, rather irritably, but by dinnertime he had thought it over and failed to come up with

a better idea. 'Right,' he said. 'We'll have them in by tea-time.'

The bathing pond, in its corrugated-iron building, was a brown, brackish square of water filled from an even more brackish pool called the Witches' Pond. Round the walls were boards with the names of those who had swum right round the pond, a distance of about twenty yards, if that. It was not enough to go round in the course of a bathing session. It had to be done alone, before the assembled day-room, with either the Warden or Miss McKee as witness. Once the swimmer touched down, successful, a great cheer went up, and the victor was given half a crown—an immense sum in those days.

I never made it—I found I hadn't the confidence—and I like to blame it on the fact that my swimming career was cut short by the fire. However, shelter is more necessary than swimming, and things had to move fast. The pond was drained and scrubbed, slatted ventilators were let into the walls, and a platform was built over the slanting shallow, with wooden steps down to the deep end. In one corner a curtain was rigged up for the Matron's accommodation, and once again began the task of taking up our beds and walking.

We quickly adapted to pond life. It was rather like living at the bottom of a lock. There was no light or heat, but it was summer, and we hoped to have part of the old building patched up by autumn.

When Matron went off after eight o'clock to sit with the other matrons at the West Block we could talk as much as we wanted, but, to keep us as quiet as possible, reading in bed was encouraged. The library book issued to me was *The Wide, Wide World,* and it was pleasant to wallow in the rather weepy fiction as the daylight faded. Sometimes it rained, a cosy sound as the drops drummed on the iron roof; and then at ten o'clock Matron would come back, and light her candle, and we would watch her enormous shadow as she prepared for bed. She had little enough privacy, but to us the curtained corner and the candle flame were symbols of the privileges of age.

The fire marked the end of an era at the orphanage, the era of ghosts and gaslight. Very soon we began to convince ourselves that it had not been a disaster at all. It was a chance to expand, to modernise. The damage amounted to £20,000, and we needed more than that to raise and equip a better building.

This was the kind of challenge that Wolfie liked. He was a worthy successor to Canon Jupp, the Founder, who had started off by bringing four children to a cottage by the River Lour, and begged all over Speyside and beyond for the money to build the present large home and church. 'Jupp's Bairns', they called the orphans in those days, a term which was alternately kindly and derogatory.

Wolfie, a canon himself by this time, launched a massive appeal, by preaching and in the magazine, and he got every penny that he asked for. (He suggested once that his epitaph should read, 'At last the beggar died.')

He also acquired large quantities of clothes, to replace those that had been lost, and the result of this was that we began to look less like orphans. We never again resorted to the economy of running up our own clothes from wholesale, bulk-bought material. I found myself walking out on Sundays in a green herring-bone coat with fawn lapels and *green stockings*! If people hadn't kept on telling me how smart I was, I might have liked the outfit. As it was, I felt it made me look like a frog.

As the clothes parcels nearly all included shoes, no one believing it possible that girls still wore heavy boots, it was decided that we could all have a pair for Sundays, and a pair of gym shoes as well, for Guides and dances. Apart from the pinafores, then, the only thing that now stamped us as orphanage children was our hats. On Sundays we had new navy-blue felts, that made tight rings on our fore-heads, and instead of the tammies we were given black berets so that the precious new hats need not be spoiled in the rain.

In so many little ways there were signs of a lessening of the institutional stranglehold. The small boys still had cropped heads, but the seniors were allowed to grow their hair so that they were not branded when they went out into the world. The girls, conversely, cut their long hair and spent hours trying to coax it into different styles. We were not allowed to wear make-up, though odd dabs of powder did appear on occasions, but some of the staff had been heard to say that we ought to be taught these things so that we didn't make a mess of ourselves when we were let loose at the cosmetics counter.

I think myself it might have been wise. The difference between orphanage girls and those outside was still too great. We knew next to nothing about sex, and it was no-body's job to enlighten us. Information was passed from ear to ear, in corners, and the facts we disbelieved were usually the correct ones. Granted, this was pretty general, at that time, but we at the orphanage were particularly vulnerable. Our farewell lecture on the facts of life con-sisted of a mumbled, 'Er—do you know about . . . ?' We usually mumbled an equally embarrassed 'Yes, ma'am,' though often we didn't know, and were dying to ask. This was countered by a relieved 'Oh, well, then . . . !' And that was that.

Slowly, we widened our horizons. The village Guides asked us to their parties, and we asked them back. The boys went for a protracted trek instead of a standing camp. Best of all, the Warden made a great attempt to launch a 'Birth-day aunt or uncle scheme'. There were so many children with no one to write to them, children who received no letter or present from one year to another. Surely someone might take the time to write occasionally to a special child, and remember him, if only by a card, on birthdays and Christmases.

The scheme prospered. Later, children went off regularly for holidays with their adoptive relations. At this stage the time was not yet ripe for these developments, but in the light of what followed it may be as well to remember that Canon Wolfe started the idea.

Looking back on his career, from start to finish, one sees so many reforms, so many humanising touches, because Canon Wolfe was a forward-looking man, a man who was never content to let things stagnate. That is why I think that if he had been a young man when future changes were mooted, I believe he would have been behind them, if he had been convinced that they were best for the children.

One of his new ideas after the fire was to start country-dancing classes.

I can't think what triggered this off. It may have been that he felt we should learn some of the social graces, in which case it might have been better to get our ballroom dancing up to date. It may have been that someone had offered to sponsor our lessons; Wolfie never passed up a free offer. Whatever it was, it was a pity that the boys objected. The girls were keen enough. We had had country dancing at the Guides, and we could do Petronella with the best of them; but the boys thought it cissy. Who wanted to stay in on summer evenings and learn to dance?

We, of course, had our own incentive. We were to have a dancing *master*, and we were at the age to speculate eagerly about any new male. We pictured him as tall, delicate-looking, palely handsome; a slender young man with wavy hair and flying legs like scissors. Mixed up with this picture was the image of a ballet dancer, someone who would hold us in languorous poses, or lift us lightly to his shoulder, petticoats, pinafores and all.

The boys stamped in soullessly. They scowled and hung

back as we changed into our gym shoes, and we decided
to ignore them. If they didn't want to dance with us, we
would do without them. We would have Mr. Halley all to
ourselves.

There was a sudden clapping of hands, and we all froze
into silence. A second later our spirits dropped. Mr. Halley
was small, bald and red-faced, a dear little man, a sweet
little man, but not the type to intrude on our dreams. The
reluctant boys began to seem interesting again.

'Now!' said Mr. Halley, in a soft, kind voice. 'I want
you all to skip in a circle like *this*!' He pointed his toes and
began to trip round as lightly as a piece of thistledown.
'*One* two three, *one* two three!' he twittered, leaping along,
his hands holding his coat tails, his head on one side. We
clutched our pinafores primly, and followed him.

The boys were not so co-operative. They stumped about,
their feet flat, giving an odd hitch when Mr. Halley's '*One*
two three!' became more urgent. 'No, boys, no! Look at
me! Look at the girls!' The little feet twinkled, the hands
clapped hopefully. He was a darling, a little sugar plum of
a man, but he had no sex appeal at all.

If the boys found the hop and skip difficult, the pas-de-
bas was disastrous. 'Point your toes! Knees out!' Mr.
Halley bounced lightly, his head nodding to the rhythm.
The boys thudded heavily, almost paralytic with resistance.

Anyone else would have lost his temper. Not Mr. Halley.
Even when a catapult was brought into the hall, and a
wad of wet paper brought him up short as he demon-
strated a curtsey, he remained sweet and amiable. 'Now,
now, boys! Pay attention!' he piped. We wanted to
laugh, but in spite of ourselves we admired him, and hoped
that he would not associate us with our graceless partners.

I can't remember how partners were arranged, but when
we did eventually proceed to actual dancing I found myself paired off with a boy whose talent for this sort of thing
was minimal. We did have a certain amount in common.

We were in the same class at school, we both wore glasses, the same rather bent, wire-rimmed spectacles, and we both felt rather sorry for our dancing master.

'It's a shame,' we said to each other, even as we laughed, but that was as far as our conversation went. It was a full-time job trying to cope with his dancing.

It wasn't that he didn't try. He was earnestly eager to please, flapping about on big feet, out of step, but aware of it. He was always taking an extra hop to get into the rhythm, and often the hop landed him on my toes. This was embarrassing for both of us. If I pulled, he resisted. If I pushed, I made him trip. He actually did better *running* through the dance, which managed to stop poor Halley in his tracks. 'No, dear boy, no! Your *steps*, sonny, your steps!'

In time John picked up and understood such terms as 'Hands round', 'Down the middle', 'Set to partners' or 'Cast off', but he could *not* master the pousette. Mr. Halley made us walk through it, reciting the instructions.

'Away from the centre! Half turn!
Up or down! Half turn!
Into the centre! *Rightabout* turn!
Break away! Break away!'

John recited it like a zombie, but any attempt at applying the formula seemed to muddle him. We must have looked a grotesque pair, wrestling away with our bent spectacles and red faces.

I did my serious dancing without him. Mr. Halley, optimistically, had decided to enter a team for the Moray Musical Festival, and eight girls were chosen to represent the 2nd Aberlour Guides. I was in the tantalising position of eighth reserve. Short of poisoning the whole team, I had no chance of competing, but I had to attend every practice. We danced 'Roxburgh Castle' till our calves ached, and we heard the tune in our sleep; and then Mr. Halley said that we had improved a lot, but we had a long way to go before he would be satisfied. There was quite a steely streak in the man, after all, but it only showed with those who were good enough to deserve criticism. The boys, he said, were 'Very nice. Very good. I can see you're trying.'

The team went off to Elgin, taking the first two reserves with them, and came in second. Somehow or other, they had started off on the wrong foot, and syncopated all the way through—a much more difficult feat, I should imagine, than dancing to the music! It was more than we had expected. We had been told so often that we must be sporting about losing that every girl had a brave grin fixed long before the adjudication. Mr. Halley, crimson with pleasure, gripped everybody's hand, said they were the best team of workers he had ever met, and that he was very, very grateful. There were great promises of meeting again next year, but we never saw him again. The country-dancing classes were not resumed. We were left with a framed certificate in the dayroom, a large repertoire of dances, and the ability to push the most stubborn of partners through a pousette.

8

The new wing

THE mornings were growing nippy, the nights were drawing in, and there was a faint dampness over everything.
It was time to move to warmer quarters. One evening our
beds were dismantled, yet again, and moved over to what
was left of the East Block. These were the old Rectory
quarters, patched up and made habitable for the winter,
and after the bare stone floor and the iron walls of the pond
it was unbelievably luxurious. The central heating was on,
there was a fire in the dayroom, and we could have hot
baths without trailing up to the West Block.

No sooner were we settled in than we were hit by a 'flu
epidemic which practically paralysed both orphanage and
village life.

To a certain extent, illness at the orphanage was an in-
dulgence, and for a short-term boost to our standard of
living, a spell in the infirmary was a great consolation. Our
infirmary was small and antiquated, with only two wards,
with four beds in each, but what it lacked in opulence it
made up in cosiness. The fireplace actually had a rug in
front of it, with a basket chair and one or two stools, and
sometimes, if Nurse had time, and was in a good mood, she
would tell us stories about the drunks who turned up when
she was on Casualty in Dundee Royal Infirmary. If you
were convalescent you might be sent to the dairy for the
cream; and at other times you could talk to the working
girl who had to clean the mortuary, and who said every
week that she'd die if she had to do it again. Once, when
I was off school with an abscess on my cheekbone, I volun-

D

teered to do the job for her, so that I could see inside, but Nurse told me that if I was as fit as all that it was time I was back at school.

Our greatest hope was to take appendicitis, or something that needed an operation, because that meant going to Gray's Hospital in Elgin, and being visited, with flowers and fruit thrown in, by the top brass of the staff. The really ill patients were nursed with great devotion, but Nurse didn't believe in spoiling us. Minor ills like cuts and scabs and bilious turns were treated rather brusquely. How otherwise could one person have got through the list single-handed? Patients had to report to the infirmary at a quarter past seven in the morning, and Nurse dressed all our wounds and sores and made snap diagnoses by candle-light. On a table by her side were lint and bandages and seven-pound jamjars full of ointment, yellow for eyes, white for faces, and plenty of iodine for cuts and chilblains. Tooth-ache was treated with a wad of cotton wool dipped in oil of cloves, and on Friday the patient was summoned from school to meet the dentist who called at eleven o'clock.

After breakfast the medicines were handed out, cough mixture, cod-liver oil for the chesty patients, and chemical food for the anaemic. There was switched egg and milk or beef tea for the delicate at mid-morning—I never got so much as a sniff at it—and Epsom salts or cascara for the constipated. If you just 'felt sick' or 'didn't know what was wrong' the remedy was castor oil, with no refinements like orange juice or a biscuit to help it over. A brimming tablespoonful was pushed into the reluctant mouth with a slick upward tilt, and a peremptory *'Bring it up and you get double!'* Two seconds later the patient would pronounce herself cured, and be off round the corner.

Now, two nurses and an overworked village doctor had to look after both matrons and children who were going down by the dozen. The infirmary filled up immediately with the more serious cases, and the others sweated and

ached and shivered in the dormitories. Some cases were
mild, and sitting up in bed in a day or two, bored and
hungry, but others took a long time to recover, and one boy
died of pneumonia.

Living all together, little could be done by way of isolation. Disinfectant was sprinkled over the floor, and the
survivors were dosed every morning with chemical food and
cod-liver oil mixed together! It looked like mouldy jam, and
tasted dreadful, but not *quite* so bad as we had expected.

The school was closed (the teachers were all smitten
too), and those who were lucky or unlucky enough to
stay fit had to buckle to and turn their hands to whatever
needed doing. Thus, I found myself lighting the dayroom
fire and cleaning the bathroom, helping to serve breakfast
and wash the dishes, and then being drafted to some of the
other jobs normally done by working girls.

'Working queans' were a senior group, from fourteen upwards, who had left school, and were being trained for
domestic service. They worked full time, and were unpaid,
but they had what to us were dizzy privileges. They ate in
the kitchen, with fried bread for breakfast on Sundays,
and potatoes in their soup, and as a concession to civilisation they drank from enamel cups instead of mugs. They
wore shoes instead of boots, and had other sartorial advant-
ages, including a 'costume' for church, a non-institutional
hat, a gym tunic and white blouse for dances, and *three*
summer dresses. In addition, they had rooms, not dormitories, and they got extra pocket money, with a penny for
church on Sunday.

All this, with limited permission to do what they liked,
outside the grounds, on their afternoons off, was a way of
breaking them in for the time when they would go out on
their own. Probably it didn't go far enough. Some of them
looked inescapably gauche and ex-orphanage in their going-
away clothes, but what they lacked in *savoir-faire* was more
than made up for by their capability for sheer hard work.

They certainly went the rounds, feeding and dressing the toddlers in the nursery, working in the infirmary, slaving in the kitchen or labouring in the laundry. I mention these last two more feelingly, because these were the areas in which I had personal experience.

Normally, I was not expected to feature as a working girl, partly because I was 'going on at school', partly because I was going home at fourteen, and also, let's face it, because even at weekends, when we were all available for extra duties, there was no great rush for my services. I still hadn't got over the left-handed scrubber stigma. However, the 'flu epidemic was a major emergency, so I was sent along to the kitchen as the best of a bad lot.

In the past I had heard wonderful tales of the pickings to be obtained by kitchen queans, plates of jelly, rich stews, chunks of pastry—it sounded like a gastronomic dream. I never got near the cooking area. My job was to wash dishes and pots, and I spent the whole day puddling about in greasy water. I understand now why scullions in picture books are always shown having their ears boxed. Cook restrained herself with difficulty. She didn't like left-handed washers-up, and next day I was sent to the laundry.

The laundry was a noisy, gloomy place, but inviting enough on a sharp winter morning, all glowing fires and red steam. A long row of tubs lined one wall, and along the other were the furnaces, flanked by high iron cupboards containing rails for drying sheets. The rails were pulled out on what looked like tramlines, and the laundrymaids tried to terrify me with tales of a child who had been caught up among the sheets and roasted to death. There were other hazards too; the stoves for heating, old-fashioned irons, the enormous boiler where—yes, you're right—someone had once fallen in and been cooked; and in the middle of the floor a new-fangled piece of gadgetry, a massive, hand-propelled spin-drier.

A picture of us using that awful contraption would

have looked like Dickens at his worst. The clothes were
packed inside, and the head laundry maid, with her assistant, would strain at the huge wheel at the side. It was
incredibly heavy, but later, as the water began to run into
a drain, it went round and round under its own steam.
The old laundry maid was most scathing about my
efforts. 'Fancy sending a lassie wi' *specs*!' she mourned.

Specs or not, I certainly worked hard. My first job, in
the morning, was to carry seven buckets of coal and seven
of coke from the cellar. After that I scrubbed clothes im-
partially—cottons, flannels, stockings and all—with a large
brush and lashings of yellow soap. We worked on till it was
dusk—there was no light in the laundry—and by that time
I rather envied the 'flu victims who had had the sense to
opt out of it all.

When I was sacked from the laundry, or the rightful
workers came back—I can't remember which—there was
still plenty for me to do, and, in a way, I found this pleasant.
Quite unsupervised, I was able to explore parts of the
ophanage I didn't know existed. One day I was told to
scrub a wooden stair by the kitchen, and I was able to peep
into a working girl's room, two beds, a wardrobe and chest
of drawers, and a rag rug on the floor. Fancy sharing a
room with one friend! It would be wonderful.

Another time, I had to scrub a balustraded flight of stairs
I passed every day on my way to dinner. They were 'private
stairs', and my imagination stopped dead at the point
where they curved out of sight. On this day I climbed right
to the top, and there, stretching for a fantastic distance,
was a long, long wooden passage, plain scrubbed wood,
with doors in the wall, so many, many doors! How they
had escaped the fire I don't know. This was where the
kitchen and laundry staff lived, but to me it was like something in a fairy-tale, all those doors, all shut . . . at least I
knew that one of them belonged to Bessie the cook. Her
black shaggy dog lay at the entrance like a hearthrug,

and made the passage look all the more enchanted.

It made me wonder what other secret places the orphan-age concealed. In a room over the 'pend' at the West Block there lived, or was said to live, a man called 'Old Mannie Grey'. Some said he was a hermit, others said he was an unfrocked priest. I never did find out. I think he existed, and I think he may have been a retired priest living quietly on his own, troubling nobody, and coming out only for early Communion. But that was too tame for us. He had to have a past, and an air of terror.

Gradually, the 'flu abated, and the patients, pale and thin, crept back to their jobs and to school. Meanwhile, behind the locked doors which sealed us off from the ruins, builders were hard at work; first the stonemasons, then the carpenters, and later a squad of Italians brought in to lay the terrazzo flooring. This was done to a secret formula (or so we were told) and no one was allowed to watch them at work. I suspect this was a ruse to protect us from the amorous Latins; certainly they used to hang about hopefully when they were off duty. On the other hand, I think there was a certain respiratory danger attached to the terrazzo process. They used great humming machines, like giant floor polishers, and the operators had to wear rubber masks. When the machines stopped and the masks came off, they used to sing together, beautifully, and we were convinced that they were all opera singers in dis-guise.

By Christmas, the new wing was complete. It seems such a short time to accomplish so much that at times I wonder if I had my dates mixed up, and have lost a year, but I don't think so. Work seemed to get done then as a matter of course, without any delays except those due to weather.

Just after Christmas, then, we made the transition, quite without ceremony. I can't remember how we transferred our belongings. I have a vague impression of standing waiting, holding a towel by the loop, in one hand, and a coat in the other, but I could be wrong. I know that we all had new beds, which was just as well, considering the bashing about which the old ones had had.

If Wolfie had been in charge of the flitting, there would have been cheers or something similar to mark the occasion. As it was, we simply walked in. And yet the very casualness of the operation made it impressive. One minute we were in the old stone passage, with the fishtail burners glimmering on the wall, and the gas globes singing in the dayroom, and then, quite suddenly, everything was bright. Electric lights shone on the broad terrazzo where the Italians had worked. Electric lights shone everywhere. Our dayroom was brilliant, and more than brilliant. The polished floor gleamed, the seats were of polished wood, and along one wall was a double row of lockers, so that we need no longer depend on the blanket kist style of container beside our beds, or the open pigeon-holes which gathered so much dust.

The bedroom was vast, one large dormitory for the whole dayroom. French windows opened on to steps down to the drive, and at once the old fears sprang up, in spite of the new lighting and the absence of spooky corners. The french windows faced the graveyard! What if they were left open one night, and the dead ones came out of the mould, looking for a bed . . . and what if we saw the travelling candle, peering by its own light to see which of us would be next to die? . . . 'Oh, don't be silly!' snapped Miss Gray. 'You should be past that stupid kind of talk!'

It was all right for her, but *we* knew that, just outside, there used to be a rustic-looking larder called the beef house, and that once there was a dead man in the beef house, and cook, hacking away, never noticed the kind of flesh she was cutting. Heaven knows what may have found its way into our soup. . . .

Time enough to worry about that later, though. Everything now was a joy and a novelty to us. The bathroom had chromium-plated taps (much easier to polish) and two showers, which we later learned to dread, because they were freezing cold, and would only go tepid if they were turned on full once we were under; and we *had* to take a shower after our hot bath, to close our pores in case we caught a chill. The fact that we had survived with open pores for years was beside the point. The showers were there, and we jolly well had to use them.

The lavatories were the most intriguing of the lot. Instead of the three toilet bowls where we used to sit side by side with no privacy whatever, were six cubicles with doors and bolts. If we'd had to pay a penny for every time we went in the next few days we'd have been bankrupt.

So far, the new dining hall had not been built. We had to have our meals in the dayroom, but through the windows in the passage we could see a square lawn, with a fountain or bird bath in the middle. This was the lawn we had seen from the old hall, and it gave me a peculiar haunted feeling, because though I had seen it so often, I had never found a door to it, never once set foot on the grass, or gone up to the fountain. It was still out of bounds, as inaccessible as ever—if there was a door to it now, I never found it—and the fact that I was seeing it from a different angle, after it should have been desecrated and devastated by the fire, made me even more confused.

The older parts of the East Block were now due for renovation, but this was to be done gradually. The nursery and the younger children moved back to the quarters we had vacated. The nursery looked much the same as usual, with its animal frieze and its two rows of cots in the bedroom, but one thing was missing; the patchwork quilts with a whole verse of 'Gentle Jesus, meek and mild' embroidered on each one, in cross-stitch. They could never be replaced. Who nowadays would bother?

9

A pen of my own

I WAS thirteen years old. More and more often, as we whispered from bed to bed in the dormitory, our conversation hinged on what we were going to do with our lives. Some of us were going home, eventually; some *said* they were going home, but most of us had faced the fact that we would have to make our own way in the world.

For the boys, this meant work on a farm, a hotel job, or life in the Army. We often saw old boys on holiday, sweltering in uniform even in the warmest weather, reluctant to loosen even one button lest it should spoil the military effect. For girls there was not so much choice. Domestic service was the answer to their problems. At that time, when depression meant more than a condition to be treated with pills, a servant's post was quite an enviable position. True, the pay was small. Ten shillings a week was as much as they could expect, and untrained girls might be fobbed off with five; but when you consider that these girls were housed and fed, and often fell heir to clothing and oddments of a quality they couldn't afford themselves, things were evened up a bit.

Prospective employers learned to look to orphanages as a source of good, cheap labour, and the girls in question saw their jobs as the gateway to riches, freedom and a more desirable life. 'I'm going to a *situation*,' they boasted. Soon, they felt, they would be writing letters like those which were printed every month in the magazine, reiterating the joys of life in service.

'Dear Sir,

I hope you are keeping well, as it leaves me the same
at present. I have settled down here well, it is a very nice
place. Mr. and Mrs. Thompson are very nice to me, and
I have a room of my own. I have a half day off every
week, and a full day every fortnight. Last week I went
to the pictures with a girl who works here. The film was
very good. I may be up in the summer for my holidays,
sir. Please will you send on my birth certificate, and give
my love to the girls.

Yours sincerely,
Emma

Behind the laconic reporting of facts lay many pointers
that these letters were indeed from orphanage girls; a hint
of homesickness, a desire to do well, a sense of novelty and
a kind of respectful affection. We, of course, did not notice
these things. What we noticed was the days off, and visits
to the pictures, the room of one's own, the fact of living
in a house as opposed to an orphanage. In our limited
experience, life could hold very little more.

Of course, it wasn't always like that. The dissatisfied or
the unsuitable came back, or were sent back, and we were
as much intrigued by their reasons as we were by the tales
of those who had returned to boast.

The girls who hadn't got on were mostly mute and inarticulate. 'Didn't you like it?' we would ask, and they
would shake their heads and pout stubbornly. 'Why?' we
would query persistently, and the heads would bow lower.

'I wanted back,' they would whisper. They would stay for
a while, until another post was found for them, and maybe
next time they would settle down.

They had to settle, eventually. It was to this end that we
were trained, whether we were going in for service or
not. The strong, hard-working types often went to farms,
where they worked both indoors and out, in all weathers.

Some girls stayed on as orphanage employees, doing what they had always done, in the nursery, kitchen or laundry, but with the added status of independence and a wage. They were usually the kind of people who needed the backing that an orphanage training had given them. They would have been lost on their own.

The job of personal maid to the Lady Superintendent, on the other hand, went to a girl who had done well at school. This was almost, but not quite, a staff position. The idea was that if you could satisfy Miss McKee you could satisfy anybody.

Miss McKee's maid wore both morning and afternoon uniform, and headed the row of working girls who filed into the hall for prayers. She had a tantalising familiarity with what went on in private rooms and studies, but she was too discreet to tell us. Occasionally, she looked away while we grabbed an odd potato or piece of left-over meat from the dinner trolley, but generally speaking she became rather upstage and too good for ordinary orphans.

The other prospective maids, less favoured, had to be content with a crash course in waiting. They were rigged out, hurriedly, before state occasions, like the Annual Meeting, and given a brief rehearsal before being let loose on the visitors. Many a bishop has had a narrow escape from nervously handled plates and tremulously poured tea. Miss McKee's maid, of course, did everything impeccably.

In the evenings before bedtime the working girls prepared themselves for independence by sewing for themselves piles of pastel-coloured flannelette garments, decorated with feather stitch, and guaranteed to last for years. Fitting out was a great occasion. What with high-heeled shoes and corsets, and skirts of adult length, the poor children seemed to have grown up overnight.

The more immature the child, the less likely she was to settle down. Thus, Jeannie, placed near at hand for her first post, came back in two days and flung herself, sobbing,

into the Wife's arms. (Actually, she should have been moved
on from Miss Rae's surveillance long ago, but she was not
considered to be mentally advanced enough.) It took two
or three tries before she was found a residential job with
plenty of sheets to patch, and, no doubt, a matron as harsh-
voiced and soft-hearted as Miss Rae to bully her.

Naturally, it was hard for us to break the ties of our
upbringing. Bella, who spent all of her time hanging about
the nursery children, was a good worker, and got good
reports, but she was for ever coming back for visits. Eventually she found a job as nanny, and the compulsive visiting ceased.

Occasionally there was trouble over money. A mistress
might offer to keep back some of the girl's wages for clothes
or holidays, and often the girl resented this, and preferred
to handle her own cash. But when one is not used to
budgeting with anything more than pennies, the tempta-
tion to lash out with a month's money is almost irresistible.
Boys who went as farm servants got six pounds for a half-
year, minus deductions, and that for a twelve-hour day.

Sometimes I wonder if these children were exploited.
Certainly, wages in general were low, at that time, but I
remember hearing Miss Davidson talking to one of her
'bairns' back for a holiday after some mixed experiences
in the labour market. 'Never be ashamed of your upbringing, lassie,' she said, 'but for your own sake, don't tell people
you came from an orphanage. Just give the name of the
last place you were at, then nobody can take advantage of
you.'

I believe it was a necessary warning. It is easy to change
your job if you have a home behind you; less easy if you
come from an orphanage, and everybody knows it. No
doubt employers felt, comfortably, that they were doing an
orphanage girl a good turn by employing her, and that
their magnanimity entitled them to a good bargain, but
the girls didn't see it that way.

'They expect you to be grateful all the time,' they grumbled. 'You work for next to nothing; they cancel your day off at a moment's notice, and then they're surprised if you complain.'

But the go-ahead ones soon learned the ropes for themselves. Often the chances were there for those who could grasp them. One girl, I heard, went to Balmoral Castle. Another went to a very rich family, and became more a companion than a maid. She had a maid of her own! She never dirtied her hands, she went abroad with the family, and was used to flying when a bus journey was still a luxury to us.

I didn't really envy her. All I wanted, I kept saying to anyone who would listen, was to be a writer.

I had already improved on my earlier reputation. I had gained my first proficiency badge in the Guides— my Authoress—while others were diligently embroidering samplers and knitting socks. I wrote screeds of poetry in old jotters, I won prizes for our annual Temperance Essay, and, with a certain relief, Miss Gray had handed over to me the responsibility for the Guide Notes in the magazine. Even Miss McKee was beginning to recognise that I was better with a pen than a duster. She couldn't avoid it. She had to read my outgoing letters, and I'm afraid I piled things on a bit, knowing full well that my father passed them round his friends.

One day she sent her maid for me, and, warily, I set off for her study. She had managed to get together a room very like the one that had been burned—a fawn Indian carpet, blue curtains, blue covers on the chairs, and a roll-top desk which I coveted ferociously. Maybe it was the same desk that I had seen rescued from the flames.

She was sitting at the desk, looking at a pile of newspapers, and when I came in she beamed at me. Flattered, relieved, I grinned back. She told me to sit down, and I sat on the humblest chair I could find.

She came to the point right away. 'I've just been reading the most wonderful story, Dorothy. It's all about James
Mollison, the airman. You know about James Mollison?'

I did. Even at the orphanage, news about the big names
trickled in.

'Well.' She handed me a sheaf of pages from the *Daily
Express*. 'I want you to read this, and then you have to
write an essay. You have to say how Mollison's life story
affected you, and you have to do it in three hundred words.
You can manage that, can't you?'

'Yes, Miss McKee.' Of course I could!

'There's a prize of ten pounds for the best essay, and
ten prizes of ten shillings. Wouldn't it be lovely if you won
ten pounds?'

'Yes, Miss McKee.' You bet it would!

'Well, you go along and read the story and then think
about it. Take your time. When you're ready come to me
and get your pen and ink. You'll have to do your very
best writing, you know.'

Next day, having wolfed down the biography, I was
ready to start the essay. I was allowed a new nib for the
occasion, and I insisted on having the dayroom table
cleared for me. I dashed off the essay in 299 words, and
delivered it in person. Miss McKee said she would pay
for the stamp.

I had forgotten all about it when once again I was summoned to the study. This time Miss McKee was standing
waiting for me, her eyes shining, her face glowing with
delight. 'Dorothy! My dear! I'm so glad! I'm so happy!
You've won ten shillings!' She hugged me, actually hugged
me, and we danced a few steps on the Indian carpet.
Between the news and the hug I was beginning to feel quite
staggered.

It all spilled out in a warm Irish gush. 'They're going
to print an extract in the paper! This paragraph here'—
she passed me a typed letter—'and you'll get your money

in a day or two. Now . . .' She sobered a little, and became more like the Miss McKee I knew. 'The Warden and I have decided that you should do something *sensible* with your money. We suggest a good fountain pen.'

It was an order, of course, not a suggestion, but I was with her all the way. I had always wanted a fountain pen.

'Will you leave it to me to choose one for you?'

'Oh, yes, Miss McKee!' We beamed at each other, and I backed out of the presence. Once I was out, it crossed my mind that it would have been rather nice to go out with her and choose it myself, poring over padded cases laid opulently on the counter . . . but it didn't matter. The main thing was *winning* the pen, not the pen itself.

And I couldn't have bettered her choice, a slim black Swan, 14-carat gold nib—'Black always looks good,' she explained. Also, it had cost an extra sixpence, which she told me she had paid for me.

The two of us were getting on famously.

I got my money's worth out of that pen, in status alone. I refused to fill it with orphanage ink, and when I showed it off at school the teachers said that school ink wasn't good enough for it either. Tommy Robertson bought a bottle of blue-black for my special use, and I was actually allowed to use it for lessons—this at a time when fountain pens were supposed to be bad for the handwriting. I wore it clipped to the pocket of my gym tunic, and at night I slept with it lying on the locker where I could keep an eye on it.

A few weeks after that came my third summons to Miss McKee. I was becoming quite at home in the blue room by now, and I went along casually, wondering what it would be this time. Something else she wanted me to write, maybe? . . .

'Oh yes,' she said, looking up from some correspondence. 'There's a parcel here for you—a book. I suppose you know who it's from?'

I was so eager to look at the book that I hardly minded
having had the parcel opened for me. Thin tissue slid aside
on the blue covers, gold gleamed on the spine. *Children's
Treasury of Lyrical Poetry*, I read. Who on earth . . .?

'Look inside,' said Miss McKee, rather impatiently.
'There's a name there.' Neat writing, with a fairly thick
pen. 'With best wishes, C. Duncan (*née* Palgrave)', it said.
I didn't know the name, I didn't know the writing. I began
to ruffle the pages, as if C. Duncan's identity might resolve
itself among the rhymes, and Miss McKee sighed,
exasperated. The euphoria of having an author in the
family was beginning to wear off.

'Well?' she said. 'Do you know who it is?'

'No, Miss McKee. I don't know anyone called Duncan.'

'Are you sure? Palgrave, then?'

'No, Miss McKee.'

It was a mystery. Orphanage children did not normally
receive poetry anthologies from total strangers, and all
anonymous gifts and letters were somewhat suspect. But
this was signed. Why, asked Miss McKee, had I no know-
ledge of this Duncan person?

'Can you think of anybody likely to send you a poetry
book? Any teachers or anything?'

'No . . .' I began to make random and rather idiotic
suggestions. 'There was a woman being shown round the
school last week, and she came into the cookery room. The
Warden told her I wrote poetry.'

'What kind of a woman?'

'Er—just an ordinary wee woman. She'd a brown hat
on. And she said her father wrote poetry too.' Pure one-
upmanship, my tone implied. They all had to get in on
the act.

'Well, you'd better get off to school. We can't stand here
and argue all day. I'll have a word with the Warden about
it.'

'. . . and what kind of time is this to wander in?' asked the English teacher.

'Please, miss . . .' I produced the book, the perfect alibi. 'And I don't know who sent it,' I finished triumphantly.

I had no idea she would be so impressed. 'Edited by Francis Turner Palgrave,' she said. 'That's Palgrave of the *Golden Treasury*.' Then, seeing me look blank, 'You've heard of Palgrave's *Golden Treasury*, haven't you?'

I shook my head, and the teacher gave me a look of shock and horror. I could see that we were all going to learn about Palgrave in the next few days.

'This must be his daughter who's given it to you.'

'But I don't know her! Neither Palgrave *nor* Duncan,' I added, hoping there wasn't a poet called Duncan I was supposed to know about as well.

As the teacher pointed out, however, I *was* late, and there were other things to do, so we went on with the *Ancient Mariner*, which I read ostentatiously from my new *Treasury*.

Next day I was summoned for what was getting to be a routine audience with Miss McKee. The mystery, it appeared, was solved. 'I've been to see the Warden,' she said crisply, 'and it *was* the lady in the cookery room who sent you the book. She's Francis Palgrave's daughter, and you should be very highly honoured.'

I said that I was.

'You must thank her right away. Go and ask Miss Keir for some notepaper and an envelope. And begin your letter, "Dear Friend, I think you must be the fairy god-mother. . ."'

My revolt was spontaneous, but unwise. 'Oh no, Miss McKee! I'd rather say . . .'

She cowed me, or almost cowed me, with a cold Irish stare.

'Am I hearing properly? I said, you will begin, "I think you must be the fairy godmother . . ."'

I melted away to collect my notepaper, shuddering every time I thought of what I had to do. I had written some pretty corny stuff in my thirteen years. I squirm now when I look back on some of it, but at least it was my own. The thank-you letter was not an occasion for corny openings. I wanted to sound sincere.

So I sat down and wrote a grateful and chatty account of my present life and future ambitions, signed it with the flourish I was affecting at the time, and felt that no one could reasonably complain, but before long Miss McKee's maid was hunting me up with the gloating information that 'she's really got it in for you this time !'

She was right. The pages were proferred coldly, and with disgust, as if they had been stuck together with jam. 'I want you to write this letter again. And this time do as you're told.'

I looked innocent and astounded. 'Please, ma'am, is anything wrong?'

The voice became more Irish. I knew the danger signs, but there was nothing I could do about it.

'Don't be impertinent, child. You know perfectly well what I mean. You will start the letter, "I think you must be..."'

Defiantly, I rewrote the letter, omitting the fairies, but putting in the odd purple passage. I was at the age when words had to be long and sonorous, and I delivered what was now a MS with smug satisfaction.

The next interview was more of a confrontation. There were no embraces now, no little dances on the carpet.

'I thought I told you to begin your letter with . . .'

I couldn't help it. 'But please, Miss McKee, it's not . . .'

'Well? What's wrong with it?'

At that moment I almost felt for her. She, too, had an author's pride, but it was my letter, a letter to someone who knew about these things.

'Please, ma'am, I'd prefer to use my own words.'

There. It was out, the criticism, the defiance, the in-
credible assumption that I knew better than she did. Icily,
she pushed forward the crusted ink bottle, and the scratchy
pen. 'Either write the letter properly or you can send back
the book.'

I knew when I was beaten. No matter how much it went
against the grain, I would have to write the sugary phrase
and put my name to it. But I still had my pride. I gave a
withering glance at the filthy ink bottle, the chewed pen-
holder, the sputtering nib. 'No, thank you,' I said, fingering
the black cap of my Swan. 'I have a pen of my own.'

10

The last year

My last year at the orphanage was undoubtedly the most pleasant. At fourteen I had a finger in every pie. I had become a patrol leader in the Guides, and pride made me sew on my stripes with comparative neatness. Oh, the joy of wearing a lanyard and an extra badge on my hat! The importance of giving orders—'Patrol, shun!'—and taking Captain round at inspection, while she saluted gravely as if she had never handed out black marks to me for forgetting my mending a few minutes before!

Every summer we spent a fortnight at camp at Hopeman, a fortnight which was a delirious orgy of food and fun and freedom. Patrol rivalry was fierce. Whenever I hear of Army 'bull' I remember the way we prepared every inch of our tent for inspection every morning. In spite of rigid Guide protocol, we met our officers on an entirely different footing from that of orphanage life. Mrs. Wolfe was our Q.M. and her jam roly-poly made us understand why Wolfie tended to put on weight. Miss Duncan, our English teacher, was her very casual assistant, and Miss Miller, of the Qualifying Class, our lieutenant. The baker was still in pursuit of her, and on visiting days their reunions were spied on with great interest.

In camp I acted as a kind of batman (batwoman?) to these two teachers. Both had a horror of earwigs and spiders, and every night I visited their tents to check their sleeping bags for them. It was nice to be trusted. The fact that I was rewarded with liquorice allsorts had nothing to do with it at all.

The weather seemed always to be gloriously warm. We bathed, we hiked, and in the evening in sight of the sea we had our camp-fire among the whins. On the last night we gave a special performance for the local gentry, and our patrol won a prize for a McGonigelian poem beginning

'The Iris Patrol is the best patrol
Of the seven at Aberlour.
We always stick in at our work and our play,
And we do good turns by the hour.'

It literally brought the house down, because the rest of the company were so incensed at our conceit that they let our guy-ropes down in the middle of the night.

There were other responsibilities entailed in being older. For example, the P.L.s used to be asked to sell poppies for Armistice Day, and at every farmhouse in our rather scattered district we were taken in and given tea. Then there were winter functions which meant serving at table and clearing up and helping ourselves to the remains. A lot of the emphasis was on food, perhaps, but at that time we didn't worry about our figures.

At school we were now in the third year. Our numbers had dwindled, and there were only nine of us, two girls plus Betty Burns from Craigellachie, and six boys, one of them my erstwhile dancing partner. We lived a privileged existence in the most coveted room in the school. It was a museum, a small room full of treasures in glass cases, a pheasant from the Braes of Elchies, a *papier mâché* statuette made from dollar bills, a snake in a bottle, and other fascinating things. There were shelves of dusty *Encyclopaedia Brittanica*, shields and spears and clubs on the wall, and the clock shifting and whirring its cogs and wheels in the tower over our heads. Best of all, we had a coal fire, and very cosy it was too, so cosy that we would hardly go out at playtime. We were not so much a class as a club.

We were studying for the Dayschool Certificate (Higher), which is now discredited, but which at that time seemed to us the highest award that education could bestow. At that time it did, in fact, carry a certain amount of weight, but as it was awarded after only a three-year course, any pupil wishing to go further on leaving the orphanage was handicapped by not having done languages. Later, the orphanage recognised this, and remedied it by creaming off the best pupils and sending them to Aberlour High School, where they could take a six-year course, sit their Highers, and perhaps even go to university.

In our day, however, there were no such privileges. Where we scored was in our excellent agricultural and domestic education. By this time we had scientific and domestic premises of our own, and the kitchen was, we thought, the last word in modernity, with a long row of laundry tubs, a range which we learned to clean with flue brushes and other fearsome implements, an iron-heating contraption which was gas-fuelled, and which blew back and nearly blew us up every time we tried to light it. We also had a new teacher.

Miss Campbell's approach was completely different from that of our previous teachers; it also differed from the kind of work we learned, from time to time, in the orphanage kitchen. We baked buns by the dozen, not by the gross, and we cooked soup in a pot, not a cauldron. And there was another thing. How she managed it I don't know, but by a certain amount of fiddling she made sure that part of what we cooked was set aside for us to taste. We had to sit down and eat it, properly served, and not only did it improve our table manners, but it stopped once and for all the animal-like scrambles of which we ourselves were somewhat ashamed.

In the third year we did all the catering for the annual
school party. We could cook and serve a three-course dinner
with ease, and turn out practically anything in the baking
line. I've had quite a lot of cookery experience since then,
but Miss Campbell's are the rules I still go by, hers are the
tips I remember. And her verdict on me, as a pupil? 'Could
be good cook if less nonsense in head!'

She made no such prophecies about my sewing. Cookery
I enjoyed, but knitting and dressmaking I just could not
master. Teaching me to patch was even more of a traumatic experience for my teacher than for me. *She* had an
inspectress to satisfy! I did eventually produce a summer
dress of peculiar dimensions and even stranger fit, due to
what I called blunt scissors during the cutting process, and
what Miss Campbell called 'sheer tomfoolery and lack
of attention', and because the skirt had been taken in to
hide a scorch mark which I incurred when I was carrying
on a conversation and ironing at the same time, I was unable to wear it for inspection later.

'She's growing very quickly,' I heard, whispered in explanation, and then, as the inspectress lifted my knitted
gloves, with odd, deformed fingers and irregular ribbing,
'And she doesn't see very well, I'm afraid. See, that one
over there, with the glasses.'

I did my best to look like a myopic giantess with stunted
fingers. 'Yes, I see,' said the inspectress, ominously, and
that is how I failed my third-year dressmaking.

So far as the more academic subjects were concerned,
we were treated like champions before a fight, encouraged
to study, but not to tire ourselves; to relax but not to neglect
our work. Hardly a day passed without a pep talk from
someone or other. On the actual date of the exam we were
excused housework, lest we should be so exhausted as to
falter in a question; and to add to the festive, yet doom-
laden, atmosphere we had to wear our Sunday dresses,
either to impress the village children, in whose school we

gathered for the English exam, or to boost our own morale.

But our morale boosting came from a totally different quarter. We set off early, on a cold grey morning, our teeth inclined to chatter a little; then, instead of marching us into the school gate, Mr. Robinson steered us into the gate of his own house opposite. He towered over us, smiling quizzically at our surprise, and there was a blazing fire, chairs ranged round the hearth, and Tony, his deaf old Pomeranian, rising stiffly to greet us. Mrs. Robinson appeared with a silver teapot, and a tray of cups and saucers, and plates and plates of buns and jam and cakes and freshly made scones. We were there for half an hour, thawing and relaxing delightfully, and the exam, when it came, had no terrors for us.

I don't know if this pre-examination tea was a regular custom. Somehow I don't think it was. Orphanage children are quick to pass on news about a feed, and this was a complete surprise to us. It may have been that we had been working under difficulties; we were the class who had lost so much time during the 'flu epidemic. Perhaps it was a colder day than usual. Whatever the reason for it, the memory of this unexpected kindness has never ceased to warm me. Perhaps to Mr. and Mrs. Robinson it was a little thing, having nine kids in for tea to kill time before an examination, but it meant more to us than they will ever realise.

Time at the orphanage was running out. We had not believed that this could ever happen, but this was the last year, the last time of doing everything—sad, perhaps, but only in the most delightful way. When the last exams had passed at school, we were redundant, belonging nowhere, given cupboards to tidy and lists to make, and finally chased off to Miss Campbell to 'find something to do'. We crocheted little hats for ourselves—mine, true to form, looked like a teapot stand—we made tea and baked scones and gossiped in corners. No doubt the house staff would have liked to get hold of us and put us to some practical use, but having just sat the Dayschool Certificate (Higher) we were deemed so fiercely intellectual that no one would have dared to keep us off school for even one day.

The day of our departure was fixed, May 1st, the day when our father would come up and take us away with him. We had known it long in advance, but as spring wore on the waiting time became both joy and exquisite torture. I can remember Lent that year, the lengthening days, the cool spring evenings, and Compline recited as we knelt on hard forms above our bread and jam and cocoa mugs, the beautifully repetitive :

'Save us, O Lord, while waking, and defend us while sleeping, that when we are awake we may watch with Christ, and while we sleep we may rest in peace.'

The blackbirds sang in the high trees, and night settled in, gently, gently.

The last Palm Sunday. We went on a walk to the moors, and lay back on spongy heather to listen to the larks. There was vivid grass everywhere, and a smell of loam, and furry catkins sprouting, and primroses in the woods. Then, on the way home, we heard screaming. It was a rabbit, caught in a gin. I think our matron killed it with her walking stick, and all the pleasure went out of the day.

During Holy Week we sang the Story of the Cross, certain to set at least some of us sobbing in great bursts of emotion. On Good Friday we suffered the Three Hours' Service, which we were too young and fidgety to appreciate. The lantern service in the evening was much more appealing.

Every year there was doubt as to whether it would be dark enough for the service, and every year dusk fell, dutifully, on time. We would take our seats, excitedly, as if for a film show. Wolfie would come in and make his way to the vestry, and we almost forgot ourselves and

began to cheer, while Spey supervised the setting up of
the magic lantern in the middle of the aisle, with a big
important boy to change the slides. After a preliminary
hymn and prayer, the lights would be dimmed, there would
be a brief enthusiastic rustle, and the show would start.

The slides were old and cracked and very familiar, but
we reacted as if we'd never seen them before. Pontius Pilate
was booed, and Jesus was cheered (reverently, of course),
till the story got so under way that we were sobered by
the awe and horror of the crucifixion. The climax, a close-
up of Christ with his crown of thorns, drew gasps of shock
and indignation. There were sobs and sniffs, and our voices
quavered over 'When I survey the wondrous cross'. It was
all far too treacly and emotional, *cheap*, even, compared
to Compline and the glorious 'O Lord, support us all the
day long of this troublous life, until the shades lengthen,
and the evening cometh. . . .' Outside, spring was mild,
and a gold moon hung over the terraces and tombstones.
My brother held up two hands in the dusk for me to count
the fingers, and I nodded. It was a secret signal whenever
we met. We were counting the weeks till we went away.

The days raced on. It was time to go to Miss McKee to
be fitted out for departure.

The clothing store was called the Nineteen. It was a
large shelved room containing piles of every necessity, and
I reported there almost fizzing with excitement. There was
another girl there too, a girl called Maggie who had a club
foot and who was going to a job in Elgin, and we grimaced
exuberantly to each other as Miss McKee arrived and began to allocate clothing to each of us in turn.

Three pairs of stockings each. Shoes. Mine were brown,
of good quality, but worn over at the heels. 'They'll do,'
said Miss McKee, and I was so taken with being an inch
taller that I didn't mention that they made me feel bow-
legged. Maggie had a surgical boot, and had her boots

made to measure, so she didn't get shoes at all.

Two vests each, and—no, we didn't get flannels. We had
been promoted to woollen ribbed vests, with a pink draw-
ribbon at the neck. Navy-blue knickers, white flannel
petticoats, and *corsets*. Miss McKee held up a pink thing
like an accordion, all criss-cross laces and steel spirals
and dangling suspenders. As she looked from one to another, gauging our size, I caught Maggie's eye and winked.
She went off into a high, wailing giggle, and Miss McKee
looked at her coldly. '*Please* don't be silly, Margaret,' she
said.

I managed to control my own giggles with a gulp and
a snort. We stood biting our lips and holding our breath
as Miss McKee hooked us each into our corsets and laced
us up. 'That'll do,' she said, leaving us to struggle out of
them on our own. 'Now . . .'

Margaret got a skirt and jumper; I got a fawn dress
with a flared skirt. Margaret got a new heavy brown coat;
I got a wine-and-fawn herring-bone tweed. I recognised
this coat. It had belonged to one of the working girls, and
had appeared in church regularly over the years. Margaret, I felt, had had a better deal than me; but I was
going home, and no doubt Miss McKee reasoned that
Maggie's clothes would have to last her longer than mine.

'Er . . . which would you rather have : a hat or a beret?'

We actually had a choice? We took one look at the hats
on display, and made up our minds.

'A beret, please, ma'am.'

Margaret got a new beret to match her coat. Mine
matched my coat too, a burgundy colour, but it had seams
which made it stick up in little points like a jester's hat.
All I needed was a rattle and a few bells.

And now at last it was coming, the great revelation . . .
Miss McKee took a deep breath and looked slightly
harassed. 'Now, you girls, have you . . . ?'

'Yes, Miss McKee,' we answered.

'Ye ken, I dinna ken fit she was talkin' aboot,' said
Maggie, as we went back to the dayroom with our bundles
in rather battered suitcases.

'Neither did I,' I said regretfully.

We were to go home on Monday, but our father arrived on
Saturday morning. 'I've got a surprise for you,' he said, as
we all practically danced down the village.

'What is it?'

'Wait and see.'

'Where is it?'

'At the hotel.'

We dashed upstairs and into his bedroom. There on
the bed was a neat grey flannel suit for my brother, and
for me a mauve dress and a blue matching dress and coat.
('Pack them away and keep them for when you're home,'
said Miss McKee, when I showed them to her. 'They're
far too good to wear for travelling.')

'Your Aunt Rose made them for you,' said my father,
and then, suddenly, there was my aunt herself, all the way
from London, hugging us both at once, and explaining
that she felt she just had to see the Abbey-lure. . . .

She really was a heroine. My father, known locally as 'a
great walker', had not thought to warn her about the
Abbey-lure roads, and she tackled the stiffest of walks in
her three-inch heels. She even scrambled up the Mound,
a local viewpoint, which somehow became translated into
a mountain by the time she got home.

The last Sunday. The awful ordeal of the farewell hymn:

> 'God be with you till we meet again.
> By His counsels guide, uphold you,
> With His sheep securely fold you,
> God be with you till we meet again.'

Leaving the church ahead of everybody else, for the last

time, the grey stone, the candles, the smell of incense, and outside, the blackbirds and the graves . . . at eleven o'clock at night I was still awake, listening to a train shriek away up the Spey Valley, and thinking, Tomorrow I won't be here.

The last day. Prayers over the porridge. 'Bless we beseech Thee that member of our household who is about to leave us this day . . .' A quick dig in the ribs, a nudge back, which kept me from crying. Not that I *wanted* to cry, but . . .

'And what are you going to do when you get home?' asked Miss Hay, supervising breakfast, and giving me the full treatment, like a condemned man.

'I don't know. I think I'm going to school.'

'Well, I call that sensible,' she said.

Actually, there had been discussions over the weekend. Canon Wolfe had suggested getting me on to *The Scotsman*, which was at that time owned by the Findlays of Aberlour House, but my father felt that as yet I was too young to stay away from home on my own. So, in the meantime, I was to carry on with my education.

After dinner came the formal farewells. 'Now, there's no excuse for you not writing,' said Miss McKee, looking really sorry to see me go. She put her arm around me. 'I'll expect screeds and screeds of letters from you. And some day you'll write a book about the orphanage, and you'll forget all the bad bits, and remember all the good. . . .'

I beamed and shook hands, but kept my own counsel. I wasn't taking any more orders about my writing. If I ever *do* write about the place, I thought, I'll write it as I jolly well think fit.

It never dawned on me that, this time, Miss McKee could be right.

Canon Wolfe was the last to shake hands, and by this time the lump in my throat was getting uncomfortable. He gave me the regulation half-crown, and a prayer-book—

I have it yet—with the inscription, 'Dorothy Haynes, left Aberlour Orphanage, May 1st, 1933, with all good wishes. C. A. E. Wolfe, Warden.' Then it was time to go. Everyone stood at the porch yelling 'Goodbye! Goodbye!' and I waved and waved till I got round the bend of the drive. Then, in my herring-bone coat, with my half-crown in my pocket, my prayer-book in my hand, my corsets killing me, and my shoes canted over at the heels, I set off for the station.

PART II

The best of both worlds

11

A space of ten years

No one who has not experienced it can imagine the delight of coming home from an orphanage, even a kindly one like Aberlour. The mere fact of being in our own house, with our own family, was enough to keep us in ecstasy for weeks. There seemed to be so much freedom. Half an hour in getting up or going to bed was neither here nor there, and we could go walks or have meals whenever we wished.

There was also the continual ritual of welcome. One would have thought we were returned explorers, bearing fame and riches, instead of the Haynes twins who had been 'away up north', as the tactful phrase went, 'being educated'.

When we went back to school we found that our education had differed more widely than we expected. The school, too, was very unlike the one at Aberlour. Teachers seemed more distant, and yet discipline was more lax, and it was difficult to know just where we fitted in in the curriculum. We had done no languages, and the teacher who tried to ground us in French recoiled in horror from our broad Banffshire accents. At the end of term exam I could answer only one question in science, which seemed to be mostly physics, but when the teacher tried to investigate just why I was so ignorant he discovered that I was *three years* ahead of the others in chemistry.

In an attempt to even things out I was allowed to drop English, the subject I most enjoyed. So far as sports were concerned, I was a write-off. Miss Gray had taught us the

E

rudiments of netball and hockey, but these games, at the orphanage, developed into a cross between rugby and all-in wrestling. In my ignorance I applied these standards at Lanark Grammar. The gym mistress was too appalled to do anything except order me off and then ask, with great curiosity, where I had learned my rules. 'At St. Margaret's, Aberlour,' I said, self-righteously. She gulped, and told me just to sit and watch.

It was all very unsatisfactory. When the summer holidays came, and I started to look after the house in earnest, instead of doing the odd bit of cleaning after school, it was decided that I would stay at home for good. Leonard would go back and study for his Highers, but I was really needed at home. I had an elder brother as well as my twin, and *someone* had to do the work.

It wasn't the career I had visualised for myself. I had always been happiest studying at school, but—studying for what? A writer need not necessarily take exams. The best thing would be just to write . . . which I did, without any plan or direction. It never occurred to me to try to *sell* anything I had written. 'You should send it in,' said people vaguely, reading with admiration that really dreadful stuff I tossed off so eagerly. And that was as far as it went.

And now, just as Lanark had seemed heaven on earth when we were away from it, Aberlour began to pull us back. My father, used to his regular visits, saved desperately so that we could all go up on holiday, and these holidays had now merged into one glorious August. We would travel overnight, arriving in Aberdeen at dawn, in time to see the fish market at its busiest; have a walk in Keith at six in the morning, when for some reason the train spent an hour in the station, and then, rather than wait another two hours at Craigellachie for the wee Speyside 'trainie', we would walk the last two miles, just as the August mists were lifting in broad bands from the hills.

Oh, it was good to be back! We stayed in the Lour,

the hotel in the square, and as soon as we had had breakfast, before even our luggage had arrived on the 'trainie',
we would race through the village, and up to the orphanage. Through the window of the West Block study we
would see Wolfie at his desk, opening envelopes and dictat-
ing letters. 'Ah, come in, come in!' he would shout to us,
and work stopped while we had a fly cup and a gossip.

During the holidays we did all the old walks, visited
friends, and took the usual trips to Elgin and Grantown;
but almost every day, too, we would drift up to the
orphanage, just dropping in and wandering about, soaking
up the atmosphere. Even after a lapse of years we still
seemed to be a part of the place. Mr. Robinson surprised
us once by taking us a run to Lossiemouth on a Sunday
afternoon. Once there, he produced the key to a bathing
hut, and brewed up a very expert cup of tea on a primus
stove. Once Michael and Hilary, the Warden's son and
daughter, came to invite us to go swimming in the Pot,
a notorious swirling hole in the Spey—an invitation which
we declined, and which would never have been extended
if Wolfie had known anything about it. Or Wolfie himself
would come round the corner in his car. 'Oh, I'm just
going to see how they're getting on at Hopeman. Would
you like to come?'

Wolfie, on his side, was a great dropper-in whenever
he passed through Lanark, which happened whenever he
went south for his holidays. He gave us no warning. 'No,
no, don't bother making tea. We're only in for five
minutes. Well—just one cup, then. We'll drink it and go.'

Two hours later, his pipe going well, we would be brewing up again, and leaning forward in our chairs, time forgotten, waiting for the next story.

He liked to keep tabs on his old charges. Leonard, who
had taken his Highers, had been hampered in his search
for work by a severe stutter, and was working meanwhile
in the hosiery trade. I had at last managed to make a start

with serious writing. A correspondence course had done no good. Mistakenly, I had chosen a course in journalism, but taken the option of sending for criticism short stories rather than articles. Without exception, the stories were slated.

We just didn't see eye to eye, my tutor and I. Technical criticism I could take, but to me the school's whole concept of literature was wrong. My stories, they told me, with truth, I suppose, were plotless. I insisted they didn't need a plot. In the middle of this controversy I began to listen to a schools broadcast, 'English for Pleasure' (I think), and there was L. A. G. Strong holding forth, saying exactly what I had been trying to get across. 'A short story should give a sense of completed experience. If you have this, you do not need a plot . . .'

I dropped the correspondence course. I stopped peeling the potatoes, and sat down right away to pour out my woes and gratitude to Mr. Strong. Not only did he answer by return; he offered to read and criticise a short story!

I sent him one called *Three Days of Rain,* thin in plot, vague in ending, but very thick in atmosphere. Bits of it he deplored, especially the stage Irish, but he said that I was indeed a writer, and that if I wanted a more suitable correspondence course ('You need discipline, but I think you are good enough not to be spoiled') he would recommend one.

I didn't take it; I couldn't afford to; but, again at his invitation, I sent him another story to read. Our correspondence by no means ended here—he was to be of great help to me in the future—but that was the last story I sent him.

'Stand on your own feet and use your own judgement,' he advised me. 'I can't find a single fault in this story. In fact, I wish I'd written it myself.'

I don't know what happened to that MS, but as a result

of Mr. Strong's advice, I sent another story he had never seen, an orphanage one, called *Tinker's Child*, to *English Story*, a new anthology which aspired to be a successor to Edward J. O'Brien's best stories of the year series. A chance volume of Edward O'Brien had focussed my ambition. If I ever got into one of his collections, I felt, I would have arrived.

He died before I was able to try anything out on him, before my writing was mature enough to try on anybody. But I got into *English Story No. 1*, and subsequent issues. I think they paid me two guineas for *Tinker's Child*, but in sheer pride and elation I must have netted thousands.

The war, to begin with, had very little effect on our family. My elder brother, Sydney, was in a reserved occupation. Leonard's call-up was deferred for a while, and I was allowed to stay at home to look after my father. I became an air-raid warden, very young and self-conscious among the Dad's Army types at our post; and then Leonard was called up, and sent to the 1st Gordons, at the Don Barracks at Aberdeen.

The Army was good for him. He was smaller than me when he enlisted, and I'm only five feet tall. On his next leave, he was almost a head taller, and broad in proportion. His stutter still bothered him, and because of this he refused promotion, but his sergeant, who was a C.A., noticed his ease at handling figures, and told him that he would back him against any accountant he knew.

'You take my advice, lad,' he said, 'you go in for accountancy after this lot. You'll do it standing on your head.'

All our contemporaries, now, seemed to be in the Army. One day a letter arrived from the Middle East from Gunner Gray, J. S. This was John Gray, my erstwhile dancing partner, who had been in the Merchant Navy,

and was now in the R.A. I can't remember who the letter
was intended for, but he and I kept on writing. Photographs were exchanged, and I began to wear an R.A. badge
on one of those peaked hats that Princess Elizabeth made
popular. Then a very brief letter arrived from a Stalag in
Germany. John had been captured in Crete, and was now
a P.O.W.

Leonard, at this time, was with the 51st Highland
Division at Alamein, and had started to write to Annie
McCarley, a girl who had been a friend of mine at the
orphanage, and who was now living in Glasgow. I had
taken a job in the local library. This was the position when
our family decided that, war or no war, it was time for another visit to Aberlour.

12

A spy on the staff !

THE village, like most places in those times, had taken on a wartime look. Army trucks were parked in country lanes, soldiers were billeted in parts of the orphanage, Aberlour House was commandeered, and so was the Lour Hotel, which we had come to regard as our second home. We were living in the Strathspey, a smaller hotel in the High Street, and our holiday fell in one of the wettest fortnights of the summer.

Day after day the rain poured down, and we sat in the lounge and talked. We had no complaints. It was not as if we needed to explore. The company was good, we were all friends together, and the conversation was gay and entertaining. We touched on every topic you can think of, but always we came back to food, recipes and past delicacies, and what it was like to have fresh eggs, and so on. Rationing had gone on for so long.

Very soon we had more to do than talk. There was an outbreak of dysentery in the village, and all the hotel staff were off. Mrs. Grant was on her own, so we all got down to making beds, washing dishes, Hoovering and dusting, all in the best of spirits.

During the end of the second week, just as the weather was beginning to improve, Wolfie came down to visit us and 'have a news'. 'You know Janet Wilkinson, don't you? She'd be about your age, I think. Well, she's in the A.T.S. now. Do you remember Eddie Smith?'

I shook my head.

'Well, it doesn't matter. He's in the R.A.F. They're

both here on leave, and they're going to be married on Thursday. You'll come up, won't you?'

We said we'd be delighted; and on Thursday afternoon, we got dressed and set off for the church, my father and I, my elder brother and his wife.

The church was very well filled. Wolfie had gone round the village and summoned everyone to the feast. Eddie quaked in the front pew, in his uniform. Mr. Cliff, the new Treasurer, was the best man. Hilary Wolfe was bridesmaid, and Miss McKee gave the bride away. Instead of a hasty wartime wedding these two were doing it in style, with organ music and the 'Wedding March' thrown in.

And more was to come. Unknown to them, a reception had been arranged, with a sumptuous meal and a real iced wedding cake. Furthermore, a wedding suite was placed at their disposal for the honeymoon. Here was a case of two young people with no parents of their own being treated as if they really belonged in a family. We covered them in confetti (Wolfie was one of those people who knew people who could 'get' things during the war) and went home feeling pleasantly warmed and uplifted.

That evening, running upstairs, I tripped and fell on the edge of the step. It winded me for a moment, and I still couldn't breathe properly when I got downstairs. I explained what had happened, and there were a few jokes about weddings, and taking more water with it next time; but it hurt too much for me to laugh, and some enthusiast who had done a bit of first-aid got hold of my head and shoved it between my knees.

He shouldn't have done that. As the doctor said later that night, I had fractured at least two ribs, and the first-aid hadn't helped at all. Having strapped me up and given me tablets, he came back next day.

'Look,' I said, 'I'll have to get up. I've to go home to-morrow.'

'Oh, but you can't. Don't you realise you're on the verge of pneumonia? You'll just have to stay in bed.'

'But this room's booked! I've got to get out. Mrs. Grant's full up.'

It was true. She was hovering about, trying not to make me feel guilty, but obviously wondering what she was going to do. A guest in bed was going to be the last straw.

'I haven't a corner left, Doctor,' she said. 'Could you not get her into the Fleming Hospital?'

'No. It's in quarantine just now.'

'Oh, I see.'

I was beginning to argue again, rather faintly, that I would go home if it killed me, when there was a familiar smell of pipe smoke, a quick step on the stair, and a black Labrador trotted in and nosed my fingers gently. 'Ah, there you are!' said Wolfie—Dean Wolfe now—taking over as usual. 'Well, you *are* an idiot!' He unloaded an armful of flowers and a large bunch of grapes—hothouse grapes in wartime!—on to the chest of drawers. 'Now, don't worry, don't worry about anything!' he told the doctor, the land-lady, and my worried relatives. 'We'll look after her. She'll come to us. You go on home if you have to. We'll keep her till she's fit. I'll come for her tomorrow morning.'

The tension went out of the room like breath from a bal-loon. The doctor said that was fine, he'd be able to keep an eye on me, and he'd thought he'd have had to send me to Gray's Hospital in Elgin. My father looked envious, as if he could have done with an extra week at Aberlour himself, and, reluctantly, they all got on with their packing.

After tea Wolfie dropped in again.

'Look,' he said, sitting easily on the side of the bed, 'would you object to going into a ward in the children's infirmary? There's no one in at the moment, and you'd have the place to yourself.'

'Of course I wouldn't mind,' I said. I was only too grate-ful . . .

'You see, we were going to give you a room, one of the rooms that we keep for old girls on holiday, but it's up-stairs, unfortunately, and Nurse Green has a bad knee. I don't want to ask her to run up and down with trays.'

I said I wouldn't dream of it. I'd go anywhere . . .

'Oh, I think you'll be quite comfortable. There are one or two of the older girls in the infirmary, but they've just had their tonsils out, and they're in the isolation ward. So you can have the other ward to yourself.'

It sounded fine. Next morning I got dressed, and went carefully downstairs. Stiffly, I waved to my family from the car. We crawled like a hearse up the rough road to the orphanage, and Wolfie jumped out like a chauffeur and ushered me in at the infirmary door.

I was back.

Nurse Green seemed to be overawed at the sight of me coming in, with the Dean carrying my case. She stood to attention as we passed, gave a little bow as the Dean left, and then, with a starched cuff, she indicated my bed. It was all ready for me, a hot-water bottle warming the sheets, and the top sheet turned back in a neat right-angled triangle. She helped me to undress, and arranged the pillows comfortably at my back.

What a difference a little expertise makes! It hadn't occurred to me or anyone else that I would feel better propped up. Nurse brought me a tray with tea and bis-cuits. Lunch, she informed me, would be at twelve, and if I would excuse her, she would go and do some work elsewhere.

Well!

Left on my own, refreshed by the tea, I began to take an interest in the ward. The infirmary was in the same place as the old one, where we had had our wounds dressed by candlelight, but the whole place had been rebuilt, and the wards were larger and more airy, with golden polished floors and pink bedcovers. The windows, too, had been enlarged, so that I could lie in bed and look at the gardens and the trees, and the rustic steps zigzagging up the hill to the Warden's Lodge. I was able, in the coming days, to keep a check on his comings and goings as he went from his home to the orphanage, and back again, but now all I wanted was to look at the trees. It had started to rain again, a faint damp smirr, and I felt I could watch it for ever. . . .

I must have fallen asleep, because here was Nurse, all starched and immaculate, coming to my bed with another tray. 'I'm sorry it's only a cold meal today, Miss Heinz, but Cook says . . .'

'Oh, that's all right,' I said inadequately. This grand hotel treatment was becoming embarrassing. And she'd got my name wrong . . . Oh well! What did it matter?

When I started on the cold meal, proffered so apologetically, I felt like calling my friends from the hotel to come and see. Boiled gammon, in thick pink slices; potatoes with a dab of butter; crisp lettuce, and rings of hard-boiled egg. 'I am sorry there are no tomatoes available for the salad, Miss Heinz. . . .'

'That's all right,' I said again. 'I don't like tomatoes anyway. But I'll tell you what. I'll send you some when I get home. We grow them down there.' It was the Lanarkian's supreme wartime gesture of gratitude.

Pudding was apple tart, with cream. There was fried fish for tea, with fried potatoes. Or was there anything else I preferred? Having eaten a week's meat ration in one meal, and having found my appetite coming back, I said that I'd be quite happy to take things as they came.

The things that came were forgotten delicacies like roast beef, *proper* bacon, and a prodigal amount of eggs. There seemed to be no scarcity at all. Having their own farm, the orphanage was able to provide these little extras, and the large numbers involved gave a greater fluidity to catering. I wrote home, gloating letters, and felt that I was coming out of the experience quite well.

Though I was alone in the ward, I was never lonely.
Nurse would come and talk to me, kindly, if rather stiffly—
I rather wished that she would stop treating me like a
duchess—and Wolfie looked in every morning on his daily
rounds with the sweetie box. 'I suppose we might as well
include you,' he would say, leaving a cake of Highland
toffee on the bed. 'I suppose you still like toffee?'

I did.

Miss McKee came in and chatted charmingly, though I
still tended to shrink under the blankets as she approached,
and Mr. Cliff, with whom I was becoming great friends,
kept me supplied with books. The bridal couple dropped
in, rather apologetically, as though it was all their fault;
and old Miss Davidson, bent almost double, sat by the bed-
side and warned me about getting up too soon.

'I used to be taller than this, you know. I neglected myself when I had broken ribs. That's why I am like I am
now.'

'How do you mean . . . ?'

'Shaped like this,' she said firmly. 'I fell and hurt my
side, and they wanted me to get the doctor and lie up, but
who would attend to my bairns? I just walked about and
held myself in. And then, when I retired, I looked at myself in the mirror, and saw I was all crooked.'

'But had you never looked in a mirror before?'

'Only to tidy my hair,' she said. 'I never had a long
mirror. What would I need to look at myself for?'

I wakened in the middle of the night. It was very dark,
like velvet, and very silent. *Too* silent. There was not a
rustle from the trees, not a ray from the windows, and
somehow the silence and blackness pressed on me like
suffocation.

'Are you awake, Miss Heinz?'

'Yes,' I croaked. 'What time is it?'

'It is two o'clock in the morning.'

'Where are you?'

'I am here. At your bed. I have been standing here for the last hour.'

'Eh? Have you? What for?' It seemed a strange thing to do.

'I was listening. I often do that.' In the darkness her voice sounded strange, the syllables clipped and yet carefully enunciated, as if she was worried about the pronunciation. 'I do not sleep well at night. Often I stand at the door in the darkness, for hours at a time, and just . . . listen.'

'Wh-wh-what do you listen for?'

'Oh, many things.'

I could see her now, against the window, as my eyes adapted to the darkness. She was standing at the foot of my bed. Somehow I didn't feel happy about this. I wished she'd go off and let me get to sleep again.

But no. She wanted to talk; and then began the most extraordinary conversation, from which I shall give only a few extracts.

I can't remember how it started, but it soon dawned on me that she didn't think much of the British Government.

'. . . and that pig, Winston Churchill . . . !'

'Oh, come on now!' At that time it was definitely not the done thing to knock Churchill.

'You are like the rest of them: deluded fools. You criticise Hitler? You condemn the Gestapo? Let me tell you, Miss *Heinz*, you have a Gestapo here far worse than any in Germany.'

'How do you mean?'

'I will tell you. They came to interrogate me. And you know why? Because my middle name was spelled differently, and was rather unusual for a woman's name.'

'And what is your middle name, then?'

'Henri.' She spelled it out.

'Oh. Is that all?'

'That is all. And yet they question me. *Me!*' She seemed to be speaking through clenched teeth. She went on about Hitler's policy of getting rid of the Jews, and made no secret of her approval. In fact, she said, she would gladly give him a hand.

I should have argued more, perhaps, but I had a tendency to cough if I raised my voice, and coughing hurt. Furthermore, I was not at all happy. She had changed the subject now, and was talking about scalpels. *She* had a scalpel, she said. It was a handy thing to have. And poisons. She knew how to poison so that she would not be suspected. I made a noise like 'Glg!', remembering those appetising dinners. Or smothering. 'You could not struggle against me, Miss Heinz. I have very strong wrists.'

I couldn't yell, let alone struggle. She would be on me in a minute, if I moved . . . A drop of sweat rolled from my forehead, and went putt! on the pillow.

'I know how to exterminate a person without leaving a trace. *A hypodermic injection in the soles of the feet. . . .*'

I don't know when she went away. I didn't even know if she had gone. Next thing, it was morning, the sun was shining, and Nurse Green came in, all freshly laundered and efficient.

I didn't believe it. I'd dreamed it. I'd been feverish, maybe, and dreamed it; and yet I *knew* I hadn't. Well, I'd tell the Warden. I'd tell Miss McKee. I'd tell *somebody*—but I didn't.

For one thing, I was sure no one would believe me. For another, it was Annual Meeting Day, when top-level discussions were held in the boardroom, a ceremonial luncheon was served to subscribers, and the orphanage, generally, was on show. Everyone tried to create a good impression on Annual Meeting Day; everyone was busy. It was certainly not a time to spring it on people that Nurse Green was mad!

Down the zigzag steps came Spey, with Wolfie behind

him, all gorgeous in gaiters, his curly hair, greying now, impressively and unfamiliarly sleeked with brilliantine. As always, he came into the ward. I had a great urge to hang on to him, to beg him not go, but he was in a hurry.

'Yes, fine, thanks,' I said.

I had a lot of visitors that day, and I was grateful, but rather abstracted. What would they say if I told them? They'd humour me, probably.

In the afternoon I was talking to a rather nice young curate when the doctor came in; the lady doctor, this time. 'No, don't go,' she said to the young man. 'I just came in to say hello.' She looked at me, rather more seriously. 'Are you all right?'

'Yes, I think so,' I said.

'You look a bit . . . Have you had many visitors today?'

'Three bishops, the Primus and the Dean,' I told her.

'God!' said the curate, 'that would kill me!'

The doctor got her thermometer out, and took my temperature. It was up a little, not much, but enough to cause her concern. 'You've probably had too much excitement,' she decided. 'I'll give Nurse something to give you tonight, to make you sleep.'

'No!' I wanted to scream. I wouldn't *dare* to sleep again, and as for letting Nurse give me pills . . . ! But again I said nothing. Over and over again I was trying to convince myself that I had dreamed it all. But I hadn't.

As time went on, I had more peculiar encounters with Nurse Green. There was the morning she addressed me coldly as she brought me my breakfast. 'You need not think you have fooled me, Miss Heinz. I know what you were up to last night.'

'Me? What was I up to?' I didn't know what she was talking about.

'You tried to pretend you were walking in your sleep. *I* know better. You knew exactly what you were doing.'

'You mean . . . I was walking in my sleep?'

'You thought that was what I would think.'

'But . . .' How could I argue? What was I arguing about?
She refused to discuss the matter any further, and to this
day I don't know whether I walked in my sleep or whether
she was trying to frighten me.

We did have normal conversations, quite interesting, if
you like details of operations and haemorrhages and such.
I gathered that she had been very ill, more than once in
her life; nearly all her stomach had been removed, and she
had a tubercular knee. She was also interested in what I
was reading—in this case, a Penguin collection of Scottish
short stories. 'Will you lend it to me?' she asked. 'The
Scottish will help to improve my vocabulary.'

Now why should she want to improve her Scottish vocabulary?

Gradually, I came to the conclusion that she was a sadist.
Her sense of humour was twisted, to say the least. When
she played draughts she liked to give me an odd punch in
the ribs, and even when she pulled her punches she would
make me jerk back suddenly, which was not exactly thera-
peutic. She told me that she herself would remove the
strapping from my ribs—'Oh yes, my lady, I will make you
scream!'

And then there was the episode of the kittens.

Two girls went past one evening with some kittens from
the farm. Nurse Green didn't like cats, but I did, and the
girls brought them in for me to see. Nurse looked at them
playing on my bed, and sent to the kitchen for a saucer
of milk.

'Now!' she ordered. 'Drink it all or you'll get castor
oil!'

They did their best, but they were very tiny kittens,
and couldn't take much. 'Drink, I tell you!' said Nurse,
holding their nostrils under till they were nearly
drowned.

Furiously, I removed the saucer, and got one of the girls

to empty it down the lavatory. 'Come and play, then!' said Nurse, taking up the little things and throwing them at the curtains, where they clung in terror. 'Come on, then. *Up* you go!' I got out of bed, gathered up the kittens, and gave them to the loudly protesting girls. 'And I've a good mind to report you to the Warden,' I said.

It quietened her so quickly that it was a pity I didn't threaten her with exposure about everything else. She didn't want the Dean to think badly of her. She valued his good opinion. She didn't like men, she said, but the Dean was a gentleman. We agreed to let the matter drop; but there were other things, and I should have complained about them too. A girl ran a splinter deep into her hand, and had to be taken to Gray's Hospital to have it removed. 'Never mind,' I said, as she sat crying in the ward, waiting for the taxi, 'you won't feel a thing. They'll give you an anaesthetic.'

'No, they won't,' she sobbed. 'Nurse says they'll just hold me down and cut it open.'

Why didn't I speak? Well . . . I don't know. She was an efficient nurse, very thorough, and, strange as it may seem, good company, in a rather macabre way. And I had become so accustomed to people telling me I had a 'great imagination' that I was afraid no one would believe me. Everyone else was so wholesome, so normal, so kind, that I just couldn't bring the conversation round to my very dramatic suspicions. Anyway, I thought, someone else would have noticed it by now.

I was getting better. The doctor said I could get up. Nurse said I could go out, but not far. 'Today only as far as the mortuary. Tomorrow as far as the graveyard.'

Typical!

In all my years at the orphanage I had never been inside the mortuary. Here now was my chance. The working girl was going to clean it, and, as ever, was afraid of the task. I said I'd keep her company.

This working girl was a replacement for the official one, who was next door in the isolation ward, recovering from her tonsillectomy. She was the most maddening and inefficient little brat I'd ever seen. I used to lie in bed and fume to myself at the way she spread polish on the floor like butter and then wondered why it didn't shine. One day Nurse hauled her screaming and kicking to the dispensary, and dosed her forcibly with castor oil. I lay quaking, almost sick with sympathy—and yet, grudgingly, I could see Nurse's point.

The mortuary, after all, was a harmless little place, a simple bier, and an altar with two candles and a crucifix. The crucifix, though, fascinated me. It was made of brass, and the Christ was all twisted and tortured, the little beard jutting awry, the spindly knees drawn up in agony.

The working girl looked at it critically.

'It's a' Brasso in the cracks,' she said, belatedly particular. 'I'll hae to tak' it off.'

The screws were quite loose, driven through the hands and feet in a real crucifixion, and she prised the little Christ loose from its bed of dried Brasso. I held it for a moment, tenderly, till she got the cross polished up, and then she went to work on the figure, very, very slowly and thoroughly. Time was nothing to the girl. She hadn't even swept the floor when Nurse came back, ready to lock up.

Nurse glared at her, and in some strange way I felt that I was included in her rage. 'You should have been finished long ago. What have you been doing? You stupid girl! Put that thing back immediately . . . !'

'That thing' was the figure of Christ, and the girl, sitting on the grass with her polish and dusters, had put the screws down beside her. Now they were lost. We all started to hunt among the grass and clover, and at last we found them. 'Give them to me!' said Nurse, and viciously, venomously, she began to twist them in. Oh God! I thought, she really is crucifying him!

A few days before I went away I had company in the bed next to me, a little girl called Mary, with burnt fingers, just home from the Fleming Hospital. 'I'm glad you're beside me,' she confided, as we settled for the night. 'I'm scared of the dark.'

'Oh, there's nothing to be scared of,' I said, wishing I believed it.

On my last night Nurse went into action.

It started with a friendly little chat around midnight, a talk about children's pranks. Little Mary enjoyed it at first. She enjoyed, too, Nurse's tales about how she used to hide behind tombstones and frighten people. 'I gave a man a fear once,' she boasted. 'He died of a heart attack. Sorry? Not me. I enjoyed it.' She went on and on, and Mary, worn out and over-stimulated, became more and more nervous. Suddenly Nurse turned round and threw a pillow at her face. The child went into hysterics, and I felt I'd had enough.

'That was a stupid thing to do! You've no right to frighten her . . .'

At that moment Miss McKee arrived.

The hysterics stopped. Nurse sprang to attention. 'And what are you doing here at this time of night, Nurse?' asked Miss McKee.

'I was just going to remove Miss Heinz's plaster.'

'Well, that can wait till morning, surely. You can go now.'

Here was my chance, when she was practically caught in the act. But Miss McKee had not come to check on her kinky staff. She was here with an invitation.

'You're going home tomorrow? Well, the Warden and I are catching the six o'clock train to Aberdeen. We wondered if you'd like to set off earlier and travel with us? You'd have an hour or two to wait at Aberdeen, but you'd have our company going in . . .'

I said I'd enjoy that.

'You're sure you feel able to get up early?'

'Oh, yes, Miss McKee!' The earlier the better.

'Well, I'll call you myself. You can have breakfast with us.'

At breakfast, and in the train, I thought of taking Wolfie aside and confiding in him, but he loaded me with magazines and chocolate, and . . . no. I couldn't. I held my peace.

It was a year or two later that the subject came up. We were on holiday again, having supper at the Dean's, and he was keeping us entertained, as usual.

'Now here's something that will amuse you, Dorothy. You might be able to use it in a story, or something. During the war, as you know, we couldn't get staff. We had to be content with what the Labour Exchange "directed" to us, and, believe me, they sent us some real honeys! We had a typist once, a Czech refugee, who couldn't type at all. She wandered about with her little dog making puddles all over the place. One day she grabbed me by the arm as she was passing. "Oh, Warden!" she said, "I'm so afraid! *Do you know you have a German spy on the staff?*'

I laughed. 'A spy? Who was she?'

Wolfie sucked at his pipe. 'Nurse Green. I say, are you feeling all right?'

'Yes, I'm all right,' I said, but I had felt myself turn cold. 'Go on, though. I'll tell you something after.'

Nurse Green, it appeared, had followed the woman about, saying she had contacts in the Gestapo who would 'get' her friends. As the poor woman *had* lost relatives in a concentration camp, and had members of her family in occupied territory, she was demented. Eventually the police were called in, but Nurse Green solved the problem for herself by dying before they could prove anything.

'But what would she spy on in a place like Aberlour?' I asked.

'Ah well, they said that Montgomery had his head-quarters there, and made all his plans for D-day. We don't *know*, of course, but . . .'

Belatedly, I told him my tale. 'But didn't you know what she was like?' I asked him.

'I'd no idea. Mind you, she hadn't taken her finals, because of illness, but she seemed efficient, and she was very devoted . . .'

'She was,' I admitted. 'She was.'

'And then, you see, we couldn't *get* people. We weren't priority. I felt we were lucky to get her. If you'd only told me . . .'

'I just didn't like,' I said.

Writing about it now, it strikes me that, as a spy, Nurse Green must have been a colossal failure. She acted the part too much. She went out of her way to draw attention to her pro-Nazi views. I am inclined to think that, instead of being a spy, she was a mental case, a sadist, quite unsuitable to look after children, admittedly, but not quite responsible for her actions. And yet . . .

'Do *you* think she was a spy?' I asked Miss McKee, the last person, I should have thought, to let her fancy run away with her.

'Oh, I think so,' she said. 'They got hold of some letters; and, then, she could always get films for her camera when *we* couldn't get them. Sometimes I wonder if she didn't take something when she knew the game was up.'

'Knockout pills? Like Himmler?'

'Something like that,' she said.

If anyone had told me that Miss McKee read thrillers, I wouldn't have believed it.

13

Family business

LEONARD, home on leave, became engaged to Annie McCarley, and was married the following February.

They had only a few days together. Having come safely through the Middle East and the Sicilian campaign, he was now posted down to England. Annie, having an aged and invalid mother and uncle to look after, was unable to pack up, as so many wives did, and go with him. He was sent to France on D-day, and a few days later he was killed.

The news was not sent to us direct. We were no longer next of kin. Annie sent a carefully worded telegram, hoping not to alarm my father too suddenly, because he was recovering from a cerebral haemorrhage, and was supposed to take things easy. I travelled into Glasgow myself to learn the truth, and travelled back again in a queer kind of stupor. The day seemed to be grey and silent, people moving without life, talking without making any impression; and there was nothing whatever to do.

That is the odd thing about death in action. There is no funeral, no ceremony, no moment of farewell. It is all over, just like that. It had happened to hundreds of people, just as tragically, just as senselessly, and now it had happened to us.

We had planned our Aberlour holiday for August, as usual, and saw no reason to put it off. Probably going there was the wisest thing to do. Poignant as it was, the people there treated us with tact as well as sympathy. We had taken Annie with us, the first time she had been back since leaving the orphanage, and suddenly she found that she couldn't face living again in Glasgow. She left her relatives in the care of her sister and came back to Aberlour to work as a nanny. Eventually she married another old orphanage boy who lived in the village, and she lives there still, with her family.

When VE time came, I arrived home one day to find a letter and a telegram waiting for me. The letter was to say that a story of mine, *The Head*, had been accepted by one of the little reviews which flourished at that time in spite of the shortage of paper. 'Look,' said the editor, 'I don't know whether I'll be able to pay you or not. If I can, I will. If not . . . will you just trust me?'

I did. Eventually I got three guineas, but that story proved to be one of the most successful I had ever written. I was not to know that at the time, of course. I turned back to the telegram, which I had torn open first. It said that John had been liberated, and expected to arrive in Lanark next day. Could I put him up for a while?

This was difficult. I had a week's holiday in hand, and was going down in two days' time to London to my aunt, the same Aunt Rose who had briefed me about the Abbey-lure. However, a quick wire brought the reply that I'd to bring my friend along with me. We travelled down a couple of days later, and when we came back we were engaged.

As John was living in our house, there didn't seem to be any point in a long engagement, but I held out for a September wedding.

'But why?' asked John, knowing that the Army were only too capable of posting him off to some inaccessible spot.

'Coupons,' I said firmly.

This was where I made my mistake. Recalled to his unit, John, like all returned P.O.W.s, was given a more thorough

medical examination, and an X-ray showed that he was
suffering from TB. He was moved up from Aldershot to
East Kilbride, and in January was allowed home, on a
temporary basis. We were married on Candlemas (which
was dry and fair) and spent a fortnight in Edinburgh, in a
hastily booked hotel full of elderly gentlefolk brewing tea
over gasfires. We were next door to St. Mary's Cathedral,
and the day after the wedding we attended Matins, and
heard that the preacher next week would be the Very Rev.
C. A. E. Wolfe of Aberlour Orphanage!

Aberlour had been generous to us. The senior members
of the orphanage staff had clubbed together and sent us
a cheque, but there was another present which has been
equally treasured. Miss Davidson, the little old one, had
looked after John's brother as a nursery baby, when he
had a serious gland operation. She sat up all night with
him, and undoubtedly, by her care, saved his life. One of
her proudest possessions was a picture of Tommy Gray as
a merchant seaman, a stalwart young man standing beside his gun. Next to marrying Tommy, the best thing I
could do, according to her, was to marry his brother.

Miss Davidson had retired, and was living in a tiny flat,
her attic sitting room cosy with books and gay cushions.
'I've got what I've always wanted,' she used to say. 'A
good fire, the *Daily Mail* every morning, and cream in
my tea.'

When I visited her, flashing my engagement ring in the
way that makes men wince, she produced what she called
a 'queer-like gadget' which claimed to revolutionise kitchen
work. 'Here you are,' she said. 'It does a' thing—you can
drain peas with it, stir, cut, use it as a fish slice—I dinna
believe a word of it, but you can have it.'

Thinking of the 'shows of presents' one attends nowadays, the vacuum cleaners, coffee sets, three-piece suites,
sets of china, and envelopes hiding fat cheques, Miss
Davidson's little gadget wouldn't merit a glance; and yet

this little thingumajig is still holding its own. The shine is worn off, it is rather buckled at the edges, but hardly a day passes when it isn't in use, and hardly a day passes but I remember the giver.

Soon after our honeymoon, John had to go to hospital again, a smaller sanatorium four miles away. He was there for two years; and during this time two exciting things happened. I had a novel published and my story *The Head* won the Tom-Gallon Award.

One thing had more or less led to another. Two years ago, at my previous attempt at the Tom-Gallon Award (£120 a year for two years), I had been runner-up to Jack Aistrop. L. A. G. Strong was one of the three judges, and had changed his mind about his decision twice. When he wanted to change once again, in favour of me, they wouldn't let him. However, as a director of Methuen, he took my first novel.

Jack Aistrop wanted to transfer his award to me, but this was not permissible—and if it had been, I wouldn't have taken it. However, at the next attempt I submitted *The Head*, and the judges were unanimous. I'd have won last time, they said, if I'd sent that story in. I hadn't dared! I felt it was too gruesome, but it has been quite a favourite with anthologists since.

Once the literary publicity was past, and John was discharged from hospital, we settled down to some deferred home life. One night, about ten o'clock, there was a knock at the door. There was Wolfie, in his slippers, smoking his pipe, and looking as if it was only yesterday that we'd seen him.

'I'm staying at the Clydesdale,' he said. 'I thought I'd just nip round the corner and see you.'

We made more tea, and while we chatted he finished off a game of chess that John was playing with himself. All the time he kept looking at me, faintly puzzled. At

last he hit on it. 'I *know* what it is,' he said. 'You're knitting. I've never seen you knitting before.'

'That's right,' I said, dropping all my stitches as I told
him. 'I'm going to have a baby.'

The baby lived for only three months. I think that the
period following this was the most unsettled of our lives.
Fortunately at this time we were offered a new house, and
here again our fate was mysteriously linked with Aberlour.
Here is the story, which you can believe or not, as you
please.

On our last Aberlour holiday we had acquired a large
black cat called Spider, who had attached himself to the
Robinson family. Mr. Robinson had now retired from the
school headmastership, and had moved from Tower Villa,
where he had entertained us before our exam, to a house in
the square. They were very fond of cats, and would have
kept the stray, except that their own cat, Podhams,
objected, so they hunted around for a family soft enough
to serve a cat body and soul.

They picked on us. At the end of the holiday we found
ourselves with a large cat basket attached to our luggage.
Spider behaved beautifully during the journey, and when
we got him home, and became properly acquainted, he
turned out to be the most docile and sweet-tempered animal
imaginable.

But there was more to him than that. One rainy night
my father said to him, jokingly, 'Go on, Spider, see if you
can't turn the rain off.' Spider went out, and in a few
minutes came back. The rain had stopped.

On another occasion the gas pressure went so low that
we could hardly cook. 'Do something about the gas, Spider,
will you?' said my father again. The cat went out, came
back again, and the pressure was restored.

This needed thinking about. We seemed to be on to a
good thing. What was our most pressing problem? We

badly needed more accommodation. 'I'll try him out,' said John. 'Spider, go and get us a new house!'

'Don't be daft!' I said, but as Spider went out obediently I couldn't resist shouting after him, 'I'll buy you a quarter of liver if you do!'

The impossible takes a little longer. Spider came back soon, with no apparent solution, but next morning there was a letter allocating to us a four-apartment council house in a new street called Quarryknowe.

Spider got his liver.

All summer we trekked up the hill to our new house, and fretted and pestered to know when it would be ready. With four years' Army back pay in hand, we spent glorious days picking carpets and furniture and curtains, and at last, in November, we were able to move in. It was a cold, windy site, looking away over the moors to the Ayrshire hills, and down at all the town steeples; and practically at our front door was a deep whinstone quarry I had never known existed.

Leonard, our second son, was born here, and when he was three years old we took him up to Aberlour. We hadn't intended to go there. We had gone to Aberdeen for a fortnight, to see some of John's relations, and at the last minute decided to visit Aberlour before going back.

'What's your hurry?' asked Wolfie, as I spoke to him over the phone. 'Come for a week. We'll put you up at the cottage.'

'But . . . we can't afford another week,' I argued. 'John's just bought a motor-bike—a second-hand one.'

'What kind?' said Wolfie.

'An Enfield.'

'That settles it. I must see it. Tell him you're coming to Aberlour.'

Being now lumbered with a 350 c.c. motor-cycle, John had no choice but to ride it the seventy-odd miles north.

Leonard and I travelled by train. Having paid his return
fare from Lanark to Aberdeen, we felt that we were now
entitled to a little fiddling on the railway. He was, after all,
only three years old, but boys of three like to boast about
their age. We briefed him carefully about not making
any incriminating statements, and he travelled innocently
but illegally to Speyside.

There, on the platform at Aberlour, was Wolfie, seeing
off a boy who was leaving the orphanage; and here was an
old girl returning with her child. It was the sort of situation that Wolfie loved. Loud introductions and exclama-
tions were shouted above the noise of the engine, and
Leonard, a serious little boy in horn-rimmed glasses, was
presented to 'Grandpa Wolfe'. Puzzled, slightly apprehen-
sive, he said, 'Mummy, what age am I now? Can I be
three again?'

Red-faced, I began to explain. 'You see—we—he's three,
but . . .'

'Oh, don't worry about that!' said Wolfie. 'I never paid
for mine until they were five!'

He escorted us to the cottage, which had been built to
house the gardeners, and which was also the lodging place
for old boys on holiday. The girls had rather more sumptuous quarters, but as a family unit we were billeted together. Mr. and Mrs. Hay, who were in charge, gave us
the use of their sitting room, and we slept in an attic with
iron beds and army blankets and a scrubbed linoleum floor.
It wasn't the Lour Hotel, but we were as snug and happy
as we have been on more palatial holidays. The Raeburn
in the kitchen warmed the whole house, and every quarter
of an hour the school clock gave its tired old Westminster
chime—the very essence of Aberlour.

Wolfie was intrigued with the Enfield, and promptly
hauled John off to see what he could fit him up with from
the jumble-sale stock. I should have mentioned the jumble
sales before this. 'Jupp's sales', they were called, because

they originated in the Founder's Day. Charles Jupp knew only too well that money lies in other people's unwanted goods, and twice a year, at the May and November term, he filled the huge dining hall with jumble collected and hoarded during the year. Everyone in the north knew Jupp's sales. Farmers' wives clad their families from them, people bought furniture, knick-knacks, jewellery, books, carpets, bedclothes, almost everything. You could buy a piano, if you had transport to take it away. The sale lasted two days, and latterly there was a special pre-sale session, with 2s 6d entry fee, for those willing to pay for access to the best of the bargains.

We always envied the boys, on these occasions, because, being displaced from their dining hall, they had to make do with an apologetically proffered dinner of bread, corned beef, and lemonade. We could never understand why Wolfie was so sorry for the boys. We would gladly have abandoned our hall for a corned beef sandwich.

The sales often realised up to £1,000 a time, and when they were over, the older children were let loose to 'scran' what they could among the leavings.

Wolfie now rummaged around to see what he could find, and produced an old railway waterproof, an army haversack, and a navy-blue beret. No doubt, if the bike had needed new tyres, he would have been able to supply those too!

During this holiday we met, passing through, a selection of old boys and girls. There was a very successful radio and television merchant, with his own large shop—a boy who had been a particular friend of my brother's; there was a young man arrested in London for suspected 'loitering with intent', sent home, at Wolfie's expense, and fitted up with clothes and a job at the distillery; another young man, also in the distillery, and living at the Cottage till he could find other lodgings; and a plump and dimpled woman with a slight limp—Maggie, who had left the orphanage with me, her club foot now straightened, and working in Craigellachie as a domestic.

Maggie had come to terms with life. 'I'd like fine to get married,' she said, 'but it's nae likely. What I'd like to do now is join the Salvation Army. I've been reading Hugh Redwood's book about God in the Slums, and ye ken . . . that's phit I'd like tae dee.'

'Well, why don't you . . . ?'

'I just wouldnie like to hurt the Dean's feelings.'

I couldn't persuade her to mention it to him, so later I had a word with him myself. 'Well, if that's what she wants to do with her life,' he said, 'let her get on with it, and God bless her. I'd never stand in her way.'

She did join the Salvation Army, but not as an officer, as she had wished. Her lame foot kept her back from that, but she joined as an ordinary soldier, in Elgin, and for many a long day she attended their services in the morning, and then peddled up the orphanage drive on her old bicycle every Sunday evening to St. Margaret's.

For all his sympathy, Wolfie was not one to be put upon. One morning, checking on the lads who had been found work in the distillery, he heard that they'd been complaining because they had no Thermos flasks.

'Now look,' he said menacingly to Mrs. Hay, who had mentioned the matter, 'I've paid their fare here, I've fitted them out with clothes, I've found them a job, and I'm keeping them for nothing. Their wages are all their own. I'm *damned* if I buy them flasks as well. And don't *you* dare buy any for them now. . . .'

'No, sir,' said Mrs. Hay.

He was right. Lodging at the cottage, even if the boys had paid it, was only thirty-five shillings per week, and that included unlimited cups of tea and coffee as well as substantial meals. It was the cheapest holiday we'd ever had; but—'Put it in your pocket,' said Wolfie, when we went to settle our bill. 'You've a house of your own to run.'

John left Aberlour a day earlier, with a push to start the bike down the school brae, and the cottage occupants standing, hands at mouths, as he roared along the village. He didn't turn up at Lanark until a day after we arrived. His beret had blown off, his eyes were red for a week, and he'd had to spend a night in Stirling—in a fire station. However, the bike had got him there. That was the great thing. And Wolfie was enthusiastic, even if I could have seen it far enough!

I have among my old photographs a Christmas card with a picture of Dean Wolfe and Princess Margaret talking to a child at the opening of the Princess Margaret Nursery School at Aberlour. Written opposite is the message: 'Congratulations on the birth of your daughter Alison.'

Alison died five months later, of cystic fibrosis. At that time, little was known, publicly, anyway, of this condition. We were assured it was not hereditary (though medical opinion on this now seems to have been reversed), and that it was most unlikely that the same thing would occur again. We decided to have one more child.

This time it was a boy. We called him Ian Edward—Edward after his grandfather—and Wolfie became his godfather. He couldn't come to the christening, but my brother acted as proxy, and a few months later the Wolfes arrived with generous gifts for the baby.

One of the regrets of our marriage is that our children have never had grandparents; my father died when Leonard was barely old enough to remember him. Wolfie became an excellent grandfather. He spoiled the children atrociously, filling their hands and their pockets with sweets ('Your mother always liked sweeties') and sending them pocket money at Christmas. They still have a premium bond which he bought for them, saying he'd always liked a gamble, and stipulating that, if the bond came up, it was to be used for their mutual benefit.

We're still hoping!

You may wonder if we, as two of his charges, were specially favoured, in that our family continued to reap the benefits of our association with him long after we had left his care. I think I would be right in saying that he was good to everyone, but so much of his kindness was never made public. So many old girls and boys came back, time and again, down on their luck and out of work, and every time Wolfie would let them stay till they had found their feet and were ready to be set up for a new start. He was always available, always ready to listen; and while he was compassionate, and tolerant of failure, he was equally delighted with success. He could always point proudly to those of his 'family' who had reached the top in so many different professions.

We will never know the names of all his beneficiaries, nor the extent of his kindness, but it extended to all those who kept in touch. Naturally, hundreds didn't. Many of us don't keep in touch with our own relations. But I don't think that Wolfie ever forgot any of his children. He could take visitors into the dining hall and pinpoint one boy from a sea of faces. Mention a name, and he remembered not only that child, but the rest of the family as well; but he never told us their secrets. Those were his alone.

14

'This is Your Life'

In 1958, after thirty years in office, Dean Wolfe retired. Looking back on this time, one realises just how many improvements he brought into being.

Some of them were inevitable. Nearly everyone's standard of living had risen over the years, and that of the orphanage had risen too. Some of the improvements may have seemed trifling, but to the recipients each step forward was a milestone on the way to normal living.

Take supper, for instance. For years, supper was only provided for us on Sundays, because tea was served earlier then, to allow us to go to church. After Evensong the younger churchgoers got a scone, and the older ones, with stronger digestions, had a slice of bread and cheese, so that the smell of incense inevitably conjures up in my mind the taste of cheese—a new one for the free association addicts.

The slice of bread was fairly thick—we were demons for thick bread—and the cheese was about two inches square, red, mild, and pleasantly flavoured. I think it was Cheddar, but for all I know it may have been bulk mousetrap. Only recently my husband and I were having coffee and sandwiches on a train. We bit into the sandwich and looked at each other ecstatically. 'Orphanage cheese!' we exclaimed. You can draw whatever conclusions you like from that.

Of course, it was not enough just to *eat* our supper. Sometimes we hid the cheese in our pockets, and gnawed it deliciously in bed. At others we would try to toast it,

F

perched on each other's shoulders, at the gas jets in the passage. This was a chancy and forbidden procedure, resulting, not in the melting rarebit we visualised, but in singed cheese, sooty grey bread, burned fingers and general frustration.

As the girls grew older, there were several cases of fainting at early Communion, and Wolfie decided that a light supper every night was the answer. Along with this came other innovations. The children's pocket money was increased, and the older ones were allowed to go out on Saturday expeditions as far afield as Elgin. This was freedom indeed. And on a large scale there were developments on the holiday front.

To any old orphanage girl of my era nothing will ever supersede the delights of Lossie. Even as an adult, taking an adult part in Sunday School outings, the appeal to me is in the Lossie atmosphere, the buns, the lemonade, the sense of excitement. But not long after I left Aberlour the fabled luck of Lossie Day weather broke down. Rain drummed so steadily that there was no question of anyone going out, and the sea might as well not have been there. There were nearly five hundred packed into a hall, eating their traditional Lossie fare with hardly enough room to move. The lavatory accommodation was inadequate, and there was nothing to do. While the staff tried to organise some kind of amusement, stories, community singing, anything at all, Wolfie tramped the streets and at last managed to find a cinema which would put on a matinée. The film wasn't really suitable for children, but it was better than nothing. After the fiasco of that day Wolfie vowed that this must never happen again. He bought a house at Hopeman, and now everyone, not merely the Scouts and Guides, had the chance of a real holiday at the seaside.

But the project which gave him most delight, the one by which he himself would most like to be remembered, was the one mentioned earlier, the Princess Margaret Nursery

School, a school not only for the nursery children of the orphanage, but for surrounding children too. It was situated in the Dowans, a lovely house to the west of Aberlour, and was opened by Princess Margaret herself. I went over it one afternoon and found it a wonderful place where children could play and learn in ideal surroundings. Everything was built to scale, furniture, wash-hand basins and so on, and there were toys galore, with even a shop, where money transactions could be carried out, and goods sold over the counter. 'Now it shows up the rest of the buildings,' said Wolfie ruefully. 'Still, one of these days . . .'

During Dean Wolfe's term of office the question of smaller homes had cropped up as the climate of opinion on children in care had altered. There was talk of trying out a new experiment of having, say, one small home nearby, perhaps even in Aberlour, run separately from, but in conjunction with, the orphanage, with a view to making comparisons; but after careful consideration the idea was shelved.

However, at that time, certain plans were afoot to make the orphanage more 'homely'. The old iron beds were being gradually replaced by wooden ones (not necessarily more comfortable, as I can testify, but less institutional-looking) and the interior decorations were improved. The school, too, had shared in the general uplift, with a fully equipped gym, and a professional gym instructor.

But Dean Wolfe, soon to be an M.B.E., felt that it was time to get out. As he put it, 'thirty years is a long time to carry the can'. A fund was opened for all his friends, old and new, to subscribe towards a farewell present, and Anne Tasker, an old girl, then teaching in Aberdeen, presented him with his first new car.

This was a particularly happy idea. I had never known him without a car, and indeed had had 'hurls' from time to time, but it had always been a second-hand car, bought after much haggling and bargaining. Perhaps the bargain-

ing was part of the pleasure, but now he had a new Austin
of his own—and plenty of leisure.

Not too much, though. He had retired as Warden of
the orphanage, but he was still Dean of the Diocese. He
took up the chaplaincy of the Gordon Chapel, Fochabers,
and soon he was on excellent terms with all the children
there. During the summer holidays John took Leonard
as a pillion passenger on his motor-bike (a new Francis
Barnett, by this time) on a youth-hostelling tour of Scotland. They stopped at Fochabers, and asked where they
could find the Dean. They were directed to the Rectory,
with the telling instructions, 'Ye'll ken him when ye see him.
He's aye got a string o' bairns roon' aboot him.'

Later, he moved to Southport, his own part of England.
We didn't see so much of him then, but we kept in touch.
He would write a circular letter, have it duplicated, and
send one to all his friends, with a few personal postscripts
attached. He told us once how, when the school where
he was chaplain had water closets installed for the first
time, he arranged a special ceremony. The old 'toilet'
bucket from the dry lavatory was kicked round the playground, and the new era ushered in with a simultaneous
pulling of lavatory chains and the joyful flush of cisterns.

'What do you think of *that*?' a delighted but scandalised press asked the Bishop.

'No comment,' grinned his Lordship.

Before Dean Wolfe's retiral I had already done quite a
lot of short stories for the B.B.C. One of them, *The
Oldest Old Boy*, dealt with an old man revisiting the
orphanage where he had lived sixty years ago. In it, I'm
afraid, I caricatured Wolfie, as the Warden showing visitors round. I hoped he wouldn't mind, and he didn't. He
even sent me a telegram of congratulation.

But what puzzled me was the way the story came over.
Tom Fleming was the reader, but the Warden's voice was
Wolfie's, the intonation, the accent, the quality, the

characteristic way he came out with things. It might have been a tape recording, but I had not mentioned Aberlour. The story was pure fiction. How had the miracle occurred?

It puzzled me so much that I wrote to Tom Fleming, and asked if he had ever met Dean Wolfe. His reply intrigued me. He *had* met him; in fact, his family had connections with Aberlour, and one of them had built the Fleming Hospital and the Fleming Hall, where we used to cheer the goodies and boo the baddies at our monthly film shows. In spite of this, I think he had been chosen to read the story by pure chance!

This was why, when a telegram arrived one morning, asking me to ring the B.B.C. at a certain extension number, I wondered . . . But they were not concerned with my writing. At least, not directly.

'We are working on *This is Your Life*,' said a voice. 'Do you know the programme?'

'Who doesn't?'

'You know Dean Wolfe of Aberlour?'

'Yes, I do. Very well.'

'Do you know any stories about him?'

'Oh, yes! Any amount!'

'Well, would you write some down and send them to us?'

I said that I couldn't wait.

'You realise, of course,' the voice went on, 'that all this is highly confidential? Yours was one of the names that were given to us, to help us in our enquiries.' It sounded like a murder investigation; in fact, I think the speaker had been a detective or something else in the police force.

'I won't say a word,' I promised. 'But what about my husband? I can't very well keep it a secret from him.'

'Oh, you can tell your husband, of course; but you understand, if it gets about generally, word could reach the subject himself, and the whole show would have to be abandoned.'

I couldn't bear to think about that. I vowed secrecy, and settled down to write a few pages of revelation about Wolfie.

Some days later the B.B.C. rang the accommodation number I had given them. 'Those stories you sent were just what we wanted. Do you know any more?'

'Yes, plenty.'

'Would you tell us one now?'

I think he wanted to know if I could put it over. I launched into a tale of how Wolfie found it difficult to get cigarettes during the war. The only place that stocked his particular brand was the local pub, and the proprietor was being awkward because Wolfie, as Provost and J.P., had booked him for a licensing offence. Consequently, whenever he wanted a packet of cigarettes, the Dean had to take aside one of the regular drinkers, slip him the price of a pint, and say, 'Oh, and get me a packet of fags when you're at it, will you?'

There were chuckles from the other end of the line. I couldn't resist following up with the tale about the time, also during the war, when a small boy nicknamed Goering climbed a drainpipe and threw lighted matches into a linen store, causing £100 worth of damage. He was punished, of course, but afterwards, Wolfie, who was a pipe-smoker, and who suffered from the current shortage of Swan Vestas, took him aside and said, 'Well, Tubby, you've had your punishment, and we'll let the matter drop. But, as man to man, just tell me—*where* did you get the matches?'

It went down well, and now I decided to ask a few questions myself.

'Look, am I going to be in on this?'

'Well, the final decision isn't up to me, but if I've got anything to do with it, you will. Now, just one more point. How do we get Dean Wolfe down to London?'

'That's easy,' I said. 'Ask him to come down and give a talk on child care.'

'Do you think he'll do it?'

'You won't be able to stop him,' I said.

It seemed that I was going to be in the show, after all. Very soon there arrived a railway warrant to London, and a page of printed instructions. 'Ladies should wear afternoon dress', it suggested. 'Avoid all-black or all-white clothes. . . .'

Well, the recording date was August, and London in August is hot, so I settled for a brown-and-white cotton frock, with what was then a fashionably full skirt. Too late, my family pointed out that the pattern looked like television interference!

Meanwhile, John was doing the motor-bike tour I mentioned, when they met the Dean and had lunch with him at Fochabers. 'Oh, by the way,' said Wolfie, 'tell Dorothy I've had a letter from the B.B.C. asking me to give a lecture on child care.' He was obviously delighted. I wrote dutifully to congratulate him, and asked him to let me know the date.

I, of course, was well out of range, but his own family were under considerable strain. Mrs. Wolfe was to be included in the invitation to London, but, not feeling too well, she said she didn't want to go. Her son and daughter finally took her aside and told her the real purpose of the visit.

'Don't say a word,' they warned her, 'but you'll have to go. You can't spoil it for Dad. He won't go if you won't.'

It was then that the real trouble started. Mrs. Wolfe, all enthusiasm now, decided that she'd have to have a new dress.

'Rubbish,' said Wolfie. 'You've plenty of dresses.'

'But . . .'

'It won't matter what you wear. Nobody's going to see you. It's not as if you were going to be on television.'

Hilary rushed in frantically to change the subject, but it wasn't easy.

'Well, look,' said Wolfie, trying to be reasonable, 'why don't you wait till you get down to London? You'll have more choice there, and maybe get it cheaper.'

'No. I'll have to have it before I go.'

Then she started off in another direction.

'Put on your gaiters when you go down to give your talk.'

Wolfie told her briefly what he thought of gaiters.

'Well, get yourself a decent suit, then. You can't go down like that.'

'Why can't I? Who cares?'

'I care. Look at you. Your trousers need pressing, you've got your pockets stuffed full . . .'

'I will not buy a new suit, and I will not have my trousers pressed . . .'

'Well, at least get your hair cut.'

'*And I will not get my hair cut!*' Exasperated, he went out and banged the door.

I travelled to London on a Friday night, and, as instructed, took a taxi to my hotel. '*This is Your Life?*' asked the lift man, eyeing me shrewdly. I nodded, with the awful feeling that I should have clenched my teeth and muttered, 'I have nothing to say!' He nodded back at me. 'We get a lot of them,' he said cryptically.

Next morning the dining room was full of people sizing each other up stealthily behind newspapers. 'Is he . . . ? Is she . . . ?' I didn't know anybody at all, but after breakfast, on my way upstairs, I ran into Mr. Cliff, who had just flown down from Aberdeen. Two hours later we were still talking, wedged in the angle of the stairs. I gathered that life at the orphanage was not quite the same without Wolfie.

After dinner a car arrived to take us to the television centre, and there was everybody gathered together, Hilary and Michael Wolfe, Mrs. Shaw, who had taught me in the Qualifying Class before Miss Miller, two old boys from overseas, another old boy, Danny Morris, who, it appeared, had badgered the B.B.C. to feature Dean Wolfe in the programme, and an old girl, Ethel Goodbrand, who at one time had been dreadfully burned, but who now had had plastic surgery. There were other people too; and when we were all accounted for, we sat down round the table to read over our scripts.

Right at the beginning, one of my stories came up, when I told how Wolfie had taken my brother and me to Elgin, just as we were, bare feet, pinafore, and so on—much to the Matron's horror.

'You are outside the orphanage, about to drive into the nearby town of Elgin. A crowd of orphanage children are milling about around the car, hoping to get a ride. One grubby child, a newcomer to the orphanage, feels she hasn't a chance . . .'

'Hey!' I interrupted indignantly. 'I wasn't grubby!'

The rehearsal paused while this was threshed out. 'No, but—would you mind very much being a grubby child, just this once?'

Put like that, I couldn't refuse. So far as I know, this was the only inaccuracy to get through. Facts on this programme are very thoroughly checked with the cast, from whose statements the script is written, and participants are free to adapt the dialogue to suit themselves. For example, the scriptwriter had us address the Dean as Wolfie, something which never happened. He was always Dean Wolfe or 'Sir'. The Wolfie was strictly for use behind his back. We got that set right, and found the producer most willing to listen to us. 'We don't want to put in anything that isn't true,' he kept saying to us.

Having hammered the script into some sort of shape, we were free for the rest of the evening. Mr. Cliff took Hilary and me to the Mermaid Theatre, and to dinner after the show, and we had great fun chasing around the quiet streets afterwards, hearing Cliffie's words and looking for a taxi home.

On Sunday afternoon we were introduced to Eamonn Andrews, in an emerald-green shirt, looking and sounding far more Irish than he does on television. He also seemed even more shy than we were. He stood in front of us as we sat on rows of forms, rather like a teacher in front of his class, but we were the ones who asked the questions.

'Why are you allowed to smoke when we aren't?'

'I'm not,' said Eamonn, guiltily hiding his stub in the palm of his hand. He looked like a little boy caught out in a crime.

We went over the show on stage, with an actor standing in for Wolfie, and all the time we couldn't believe that it would ever be transmitted. So many things seemed to go wrong! And here was Danny Morris in a panic, because somehow or other word had reached him that Wolfie had arrived in London, and was on his way to his, Danny's, lodgings. 'The landlady knows I'm here,' he said. 'She'll let the cat out of the bag!'

'No, no, she won't,' said Ronald Vivian soothingly. Having researched the programme, he knew what was what. 'Even if she says you're here, he won't suspect. He knows that you know he'll be here, and he'll think you've gone down to meet him.'

'But suppose . . . ?'

'Don't worry. We'll get the police to head him off, if necessary.'

The plan was that he would be taken on a tour of the television centre. Arriving at the theatre, his escort, Ronald Vivian, would say, 'Oh, we're in luck. We're just in time to see a bit of a performance.'

'But what if he gets away?' persisted Danny, who was rapidly losing his nerve.

'Not from me he won't!' Mr. Vivian clenched an enormous and muscular fist.

Apart from our natural nervousness, we were beginning to feel safe and sheltered, even cosseted. The B.B.C. was in charge, and the fact that even the police could be pressed into service was very reassuring; that, and the fact that Eamonn was so pleasant to work with. I think that everyone expected some sort of show of authority when he was on stage; in actual fact, he was quiet and patient when things were held up by camera difficulties or other technical hitches, and he was very helpful as we amateurs went woodenly through our lines. 'Don't worry,' he said. 'Just relax. You'll be all right when the time comes.'

The B.B.C. gave us our dinner—not, I suspect, from generosity; having booked us into a hotel, our expenses barely covered the cost—but in case any of us should get lost. Surprisingly, most of us ate well. Then it was back to the studios. We were made up, our faces powdered yellow for the TV lights, special lipstick applied, eyebrows accentuated, if necessary, and our hair combed attractively. There was a last-minute briefing. 'You sit here and watch the programme on the monitor. You'll be told when to stand in the wings, and the floor boy will give you a tap on the shoulder when it's time to speak or go on. Go on *exactly* when he tells you, no matter what happens. If a bomb falls, or the stage goes on fire, walk on regardless. Even if you think your cue is wrong, go on. We can always get a new floor boy.'

I think, at first, we all hoped that the stage would open to let us sink from sight, but it is amazing how another person's plight can make us forget our own. Inevitably, we were beginning to think about Wolfie rather than ourselves. Eamonn, in a dark suit now, with his face made up, and his famous book under his arm, went past, and made a circle with his finger and thumb in the air. 'You'll all be smashing,' he said, and we sat up, suddenly infused with confidence. Of course we would!

The suspense was crawling under our skin and beating

drums in our stomachs. Don't let anybody ever tell me
that this programme is faked, or that the subject knows in
advance! The opening music started, and Eamonn
appeared.

'Good evening, ladies and gentlemen, and thank you.
Six years ago, on a cold and dreary Sunday evening, the
vicar of a church in the Scottish Highlands came out after
the service and saw a little girl standing alone and crying.
From her thin and tattered dress he unpinned a note.
"Please take care of this child", he read. To the minister,
she was just yet another to be taken to his heart as hundreds had been before. Look at her a few weeks afterwards,
as bonny a bairn as you would wish to see.

'Tonight that vicar is being taken behind the scenes of
television. He's been on a tour of the B.B.C.'s new television centre. He should be arriving here at any moment
now.'

We were all clinging together backstage, biting our
nails, peering into the dimness of the television screen.
There was a quick rustle. 'There he is!' A faint blur of a
face at the door, and Eamonn hovering with a microphone.

'Good evening,' said Eamonn. 'Would you mind telling
me why you are here tonight?'

There was a faint murmur from the doorway, something
about seeing a show.

'And you won't be disappointed,' said Eamonn, more
loudly. 'You really are here for that purpose. Dean
Clarence Wolfe, M.B.E., This is Your Life!'

Amid all the cheers and confusion, Wolfie, I learned
later, had one overwhelming worry. 'What'll I do with
my hat?' For some reason or other, he felt he couldn't
take it up on stage. He threw it away, along a row of seats,
and someone handed it back to him later.

'. . . and I thought I was going to give a talk on child
care!' we heard him saying, almost querulously, to
Eamonn.

'Dean Clarence Wolfe,' Eamonn went on, 'this is your life, a story of kindness and love for one of Scotland's largest families, the children of Aberlour Orphanage.'

Suddenly I realised I was in the wings, my throat apparently paralysed. I cleared it experimentally, but it didn't help. A tap on my shoulder! I said my introductory line, off stage, and my voice sounded astonishingly clear—and rather prim and plummy, I thought later.

Wolfie was supposed to recognise me, but looked puzzled. Then Eamonn announced me. I felt another tap on my shoulder, and I was on, under the lights, so pleased and excited and caught up with Wolfie's amazement that I had no longer any thought of being nervous.

His reaction was typical: a delighted and spontaneous 'Dorothy! My dear!' and then, as we were motioned to a seat, a swift '*You* had something to do with this, you little devil!'

Luckily, the mike didn't pick that one up!

Nor did the camera pick up the emotion he showed when it was time for me to go, after telling about how we had wept for him at the fire. As we embraced, his face twisted suddenly, his eyes filled with tears, and his lips trembled. 'Oh, Dorothy, my dear, my dear!' he mumbled, hiding on my shoulder; then he recovered, and *I* was dabbing at my eyes and blowing my nose before I went back to my seat to watch the others go through their paces.

I won't go over the whole of the script, but I can't avoid mentioning one or two of the highlights. One was when Eamonn played his familiar trick of showing a filmed interview with two boys hundreds of miles away, and then bringing them on in person. As soon as he'd got over his delight, Wolfie at once asked after their brothers. 'I didn't think he'd remember *me*,' said one of them, 'let alone the rest of the family!'

But the climax of the show came when Ethel Goodbrand told how she had arrived at the orphanage scarred, dis-

figured and terrified, and how Wolfie had gently encouraged the other children to play with her; and then Danny
Morris told how, at his retiral presentation, the Dean had
asked him to look after Ethel. They had grown to love
each other.

'When you brought us together,' said Danny, 'I didn't
know that I should be saying to you, "Please will you marry
us, and may it be at Aberlour?" '

'Of *course* I will !' beamed Wolfie.

The whole thing was a tremendous success, but this was
a recording, and by the time it was sent out, and the
newspapers got hold of the story, the couple were married.

Meantime, the Aberlour Orphanage choir had come on
to sing the 23rd Psalm, and Wolfie stood there, blissfully
conducting—taking over, as usual. His trousers were un-
pressed, his pockets bulged, and his hair was uncut; but
when they showed his profile as the credits went up, I
thought I had never seen him look so noble.

There was a party afterwards, with all sorts of refresh-
ments flowing freely, and everyone gloriously elated. For
the first time in his life, I think, Wolfie looked drunk, but
I can vouch for the fact that he touched nothing but
orange juice. Everybody was milling around, signing
scripts, promising to keep in touch—it was a wonderful
night, the kind of experience that lasts long after the
cameras have stopped rolling.

'Would you have done it, if you'd known?' we asked him
later.

He said he didn't think so; and yet he had enjoyed
it. He enjoyed it so much that he found himself talking
about it, compulsively, trying to get it out of his system.
'And look,' he said, producing a crumpled letter from his
pocket, with a few sentences underlined. 'I *knew* you had
a hand in this. Of all the artful little . . .'

I took the paper from him, and read in my own writing :
'John tells me that you are to give a broadcast on child care.

Let me know when it's due to come off, as I'd like to listen. . . .'

It was a long time after, many years later, that I learned, to my surprise, that the Aberlour people were disappointed in the programme. 'I didn't like it,' they said. 'It was all about belting the kids, strapping and punishing.'

Was it? I didn't think so, but for curiosity's sake, I went over the tattered script. They were right, in a way. There *were* frequent references to strapping, but they were affectionate references to punishment not resented, but accepted as just, or punishment withheld when it was thought that clemency might do more good. I doubt if any of the cast noticed it. All I remember was the collective desire to praise and honour a good man we had loved.

15

The rundown

IT is not easy for a man to take over from a successful predecessor, especially one who has been a personality. The job of Warden of Aberlour Orphanage was by no means a sinecure, at any time, and to follow in Dean Wolfe's footsteps required a certain amount of courage.

The Rev. C. W. Leslie, who took on this unenviable task, was essentially an administrator, a good administrator, but without the rich warm humanity of the Dean. According to his writing in the magazine, his aim in running the orphanage was to do at all times what was best for the children. This he did, in the most efficient way. Pocket money was increased, clothes became more plentiful and more expensive, and the children were no longer required to do housework. Staff cleaners were appointed, and, according to one report, 'the kids were never allowed to dirty their hands'.

Regrettably, I never had the chance to get to know Mr. Leslie. I met him briefly at *This is Your Life,* and I had a short note from him in answer to an article I supplied for the magazine on the Dean's retiral. I cannot, therefore, give a personal assessment of his qualities. All I can do is to quote the rather varying reactions of those who knew and worked with him.

'He means well. I'm sure he means well, but . . . it's difficult to get to know him. He does his job efficiently, he considers the kid's welfare, but they don't run to him like they used to run to Dean Wolfe.'

People differ, of course. Wolfie was an extrovert, a showman. He took a certain pride in telling that once, on holiday, he went to a phrenologist to have his 'bumps' read, without revealing that he was a parson.

'Well, what am I?' he demanded, after the operation.

'I don't know,' said the baffled phrenologist, 'but you could be a con man!'

He couldn't help getting involved with people. Any strangers that he met in the grounds he would greet affably, accompany round the orphanage, and make them generally welcome. His successor was apt to pass them by as if he hadn't seen them. My elder brother—a sort of adoptive old orphanage boy—once took a friend in to see the church when he was spending a holiday on Speyside. They passed the new Warden on the way in, and he ignored them completely. It may not have been intentional, but it was a change from the old days—and the orphanage lost by it, on this and other similar occasions. The warden of an institution which relies on voluntary contributions has to be something like Royalty—careful never to offend.

But his greatest fault seemed to be his off-hand treatment of old boys and girls. From the very inception of the orphanage it had been the tradition that the home was always open to anyone who wished to come back. And people of all kinds did come, both to visit and to stay. So many people turned up, from time to time, that an extension was built on to the cottage, for the express purpose of putting up old boys. It was called the Walter Jenks Hostel, Dean Jenks being the Warden who followed the Founder, and every summer it was used to capacity.

But now the welcome seemed to be wearing thin. People who arrived, expecting to be accepted as members of the family, and hoping to make a new friend in the Warden, were bitterly disappointed with their reception.

'But this is my *home*,' one girl remarked, after having been turned away at the front entrance. 'I always come up. I wrote to say I was coming.' But who can you appeal to when the head of the house says 'No'?

Against this, it is only fair to state that Mr. Leslie seemed to dislike visitors on principle. Where Dean Wolfe welcomed them as allies, Mr. Leslie saw them as an intrusion on the children's privacy. Ordinary families are not put on show to strangers; maybe orphanage children shouldn't be either; but this does not, of course, mean that old boys and girls should be treated as intruders.

The cold-shoulder treatment wasn't meted out only to visitors. Even Dean Wolfe himself was made to feel in the way. He told me the story himself, making it sound like a joke, but I could see that his laughter was rather forced.

'I didn't go back for a while,' he said. 'Well, you know how it is. I didn't want to go breathing down the man's neck. But I was up north on holiday' (he was perpetual curate of Glasson from 1960–3) 'and I thought I'd like to see the place again. So I rang up and said I'd like to come over. I felt it wasn't fair to spring a visit on him. I didn't give my name, though. I just said I wanted to see the Warden. And do you know what the girl at the telephone said? She said I'd have to make an appointment. Imagine, an appointment at Aberlour Orphanage! "Who's speaking, please," she kept saying, but I wouldn't tell her. "Who's speaking?" she said again, like a robot. At last I lost my rag. "Oh, come off it, Isabel!" I said. (I knew who *she* was.) "You know perfectly well who it is. Now just take that message for me and stop that nonsense!"'

He did get his appointment. He was granted ten minutes in the office, and given a cup of tea and two ginger snaps. Luckily, the staff were more hospitable. He was entertained by many of his friends, and the reputation of the orphanage as a friendly place was thereby saved.

Again, being fair, not all the reports I heard were like this. 'At least,' said some of the staff, 'Mr. Leslie was decent with us. He gave us all a rise in our salaries. We'd been working for peanuts before that.'

It was true. The rise would have been paid, in any case, whoever was in charge, because their wages were due to go up; but it is conceivable that there might have been a certain amount of discontent in the old days over the way they were expected to do extra duties on the side.

'You don't work for money here, you know,' was one of Wolfie's sayings. 'You do it for the sake of the children of Aberlour.' No doubt he was right. He had run the orphanage for years on this principle, but while the matrons of yesteryear were quite happy to dedicate their lives thus, the newer generation were less willing. A new spirit was creeping in, and C. W. Leslie inadvertently fostered discontent with the past while preventing it from coming to a head in the present.

About this time the orphanage was kept busy denying press reports that it was about to close. What was going to happen, the denials explained, was that the buildings were to be run down gradually, and the children housed in smaller units of family type homes.

This, as I explained earlier, was not a new idea. For some time the numbers had been declining, because the trend was towards fostering children rather than boarding them in large institutions. The type of child who was admitted, too, had changed. Whereas Aberlour had taken orphans, or children in need, admittedly of varying mental and moral calibre, they were now being sent children, often older boys, who had, for one reason or another, proved unsuitable for fostering. The delinquency rate rose, and fears were expressed in some quarters that Aberlour might eventually become a sort of Borstal.

It was against this background of change and uncer-

tainty that Rediffusion featured Aberlour Orphanage in
a rather controversial TV programme.

At that time they (Rediffusion) were doing a series of
TV documentaries which can only be described as slanted
sensationalism. For example, there was some adverse reporting on the police at Scotland Yard, and about doctors in
the new town of Harlow, reporting which was strongly
criticised in the correspondence columns of *The Times*. I
didn't see these two programmes, but I did see the one in
which Aberlour Orphanage featured, and which, I am
assured by people who saw all three, was very much in the
same vein.

The programme was about the old and the new in child
care, with Aberlour being used as an example. The new
was fairly ordinary. Members of a family in one of the small
homes were interviewed, and asked if they preferred this to
orphanage life. The main advantage seemed to be that
they could go to dances!

In the programme showing the old orphanage way of
life the shots were slanted in a way that gave a thoroughly
wrong impression; and again, as in the Scotland Yard and
Harlow broadcasts, indignation was aroused. The Provost
of Aberlour, Mr. Peter Taylor, complained at once to the
press that the film had been rigged, and the *Daily Express*
featured the complaint in its headlines.

Another shot, made in the school, and accompanied by
the comment that the educational standard was poor, because nobody took O-levels, also provoked anger. In fact,
the school had consistently good reports from Her Majesty's
Inspector. It was a junior secondary school, and at no similar
school in the county were O-levels taken. Any child pro-
ceeding to such was transferred to Aberlour High School;
one orphanage boy who had taken O-levels there was at
that moment at the university and has since qualified as a
doctor.

Supported by H.M.I., the headmaster and staff complained to Rediffusion, and received what amounted to an apology with the explanation that 'we reported what we were told'.

Who told them?

Little by little, our links with the orphanage seemed to be slipping. There were changes everywhere. Even the jumble sales seemed to be in danger of being stopped. Because the rising cost of carriage made it uneconomical to send sacks of jumble, and because the Aberlour railway station had been closed, with the closing of the Speyside line, churches, guilds and other groups were now asked to hold their own sales, and send the proceeds to Aberlour. It seemed a reasonable thing to do. With Mrs. Wolfe and Miss McKee, the main sale organisers, now retired, who was to take on the never-ending task of dealing with the tons and tons of jumble? But if the sales stopped, not only the orphanage would be the poorer for it. The whole of the north-east would suffer.

As it happened, they were able to carry on, with Mrs. Leslie's help, until the end, and the wives of Banff and Morayshire netted their bargains until 1967.

The orphanage appeared to be thriving. Money was flashed about gaily. Children went for holidays all over the place, which was an enormous benefit to them. The bathing pond was enlarged and heated; and they now employed a P.R.O. who was prepared to travel anywhere and show films— complimentary ones, this time—at an unspecified salary. All a reasonable investment, no doubt—but Wolfie had needed no P.R.O. *He* travelled the country, preaching in halls and churches, begging, begging all the time, and this on top of his work as Warden and Dean of the Diocese.

The maddening thing was the way in which these changes were made. I have tried to be fair and impartial, but I can't help feeling that all this progress—and there is

no doubt that progress was made—came at the cost of so
much that had been good. There seemed to be, in all the
proposals that were mooted, a depreciatory attitude towards the old methods which were now honourably out
of date. The collecting boxes were redesigned. ('The little
boy on the label is a man now. We need a new approach.')
The magazine had a new format. ('We want the magazine to be bright.') But the new magazine wasn't doing
nearly so well as the old. 'We miss the old boys' and girls'
letters,' complained the readers. 'We miss the journal. It's
not nearly so *interesting*.' In vain the editor, who was
genuinely against publishing private correspondence,
filled up space with recipes and suchlike. We didn't want
recipes. We wanted those intimate and fascinating items
about orphanage life.

The next controversy was about the sale of the orphanage
furnishings. Jupp's sale had nothing on this bonanza.
Furniture, curtains, all went for next to nothing. The publicity was so bad that the orphanage felt it necessary to issue
a statement in the next magazine. The sale, it assured us,
had been properly advertised and conducted. The articles
had been sold because they were institutional equipment,
unsuitable for use anywhere else; for example, large tables,
catering utensils, extra long tablecloths, stage curtains, and
so on.

   In fairness, it should be stated that the sale had been
entrusted to a well-known and reputable firm of auction-
eers, and disappointing as the result was, it was largely due
to the circumstances in which the sale had to be held.

The next **thing** was an announcement that gifts and
donations would receive only a stereotyped form of acknow-
ledgement. 'In the past it has been the custom to acknow-
ledge all gifts with a personal letter. It would be in the
interests of economy if . . .'

This was the last straw. When I think of the delighted and delightful letters which were sent on the receipt of any gift, however small; when I think of the number of new friends won by a friendly letter, I cannot believe that anyone could wish to risk this flood of goodwill in the name of economy. It was all far too artificial and cold.

We cancelled our magazine.

It was Mr. Cliff who wrote to tell us that Dean Wolfe had died at seventy-five, of a cerebral haemorrhage. He had had an active retirement. His death came suddenly and unexpectedly, and a contingent from Aberlour went to Southport for his funeral.

Later, a memorial plaque was erected in St. Margaret's Church. The Bishop of Moray preached at the Memorial Service, and made no secret of the fact that he was far from pleased at what had happened to the orphanage. The orphanage was an Episcopal foundation. It seemed to the Bishop that under the new constitution the links with the Episcopal Church would be very tenuous.

The orphanage was put up for sale. Down in Lancashire a dealer who had had an eye for such opportunities noticed the advertisement, and came north through the night to see for himself. Arrived in Aberlour, he looked at the empty buildings, the beautiful mellow walls, the broad drives and gardens. Totally without sentiment, he looked at them. 'Founded by Charles Jupp, 1875 . . .' The slow saving, the slow building, stone upon stone, the thousands of lives shaped, like the stones, carved and smoothed, each to their appointed place, the good accruing, year upon year . . . and now a machinery merchant from Wigan, looking at it shrewdly, and shaking his head.

'God knows what I'll do with it . . . but I'll buy it.'

And now the orphanage was empty. There was a grand

new reception centre at Rubislaw Den, in Aberdeen, but all alone, in the old boys' hostel, Mr. Cliff stayed on and wound up the remaining business. He was shortly to retire, but would not go until the work was finished. 'It is quiet here,' he wrote, 'not a voice, not a footstep. Only ghosts . . .'

There were ghosts in plenty as we stood in the stillness, that February night. It will be a long time before they are exorcised.

Epilogue

THIS holiday, however, this silver wedding week, was meant to be a celebration, not a wake. We were treated like Royalty all the way. The red carpet was stretched from one end of the village to the other, and we lost count of the number of times our health was drunk, in anything from Dry Sack to the best of the local stuff.

One of the highlights was a visit to Aberdeen, where Nurse Munro, eighty years old, and at one time in charge of the nursery children, arranged a reunion with several old girls. We talked of the good old days . . . or were they? The miracle of amnesia that Miss McKee had referred to had worked for me, but not always for them. The earlier days of the orphanage seemed to have been pretty tough. I can remember the magazine boasting that it cost only ten shillings a week to keep a child, and that ten shillings had to run to clothes and lodging as well as food.

'Of course, they didn't have the money,' Nurse said. 'I was paid barely fifteen shillings a week. It's the only post I had where I was never able to save. I spent it a' on the bairns, buying them bread and jam.'

Affectionate reminiscences vied with more measured assessment. There is no doubt that, in some circumstances, an orphanage background can be a handicap. I personally have never found it so (though I haven't had to stress it) but some of my fellow guests had not been so fortunate. Some of them, mothers and even grandmothers, prefer to keep their orphanage origins dark. 'It just wouldn't do,'

they say, or 'Well, I don't mind, but the children do. You've
to keep quiet for their sake.'

Ours don't mind. We asked them, later, remembering
this point, but they seemed surprised at the question. They
do occasionally get exasperated at our way of going into
reminiscent huddles, or our parental nagging, 'If you had
spent two or three years at the orphanage . . .' but that
is all. Perhaps the parents' attitude reacts on the children.

Maybe the smaller homes will remove this institutional
stigma. I haven't seen any of the new Aberlour Homes,
because, unlike the old orphanage, they do not encourage
casual visitors. However, the new regime was fully discussed
in the village.

'Well, we were invited to Rubislaw Den, and it's got to
be seen to be believed. Thick carpets, gorgeous curtains—
any normal child would be scared stiff. It almost scared
me!'

'Luxury just isn't the word for it. But what's it all *for*?
The kids aren't in it for more than a few days. It's only a
reception centre.'

'I don't see why they need a reception centre anyway.'

'Well, if the homes are furnished on the same scale, they
must be going mad with their money. It's going to be
tough on the children when they go out on their own.'

It was tough on us, too. In spite of our more Spartan
upbringing, our life had been sheltered, but at least we,
who had had so little, knew how to make the best of what
we had. The trend nowadays (though I feel diffident about
saying this) seems to be to overcompensate for the lack of
parents and a normal home. I would suggest that deprived children need not so much material comforts as
warmth and loving kindness. There is no reason, of course,
why they shouldn't have both, and no suggestion that one
takes the place of the other in the new homes, but those

who knew the orphanage in our time (and many who didn't) feel that the present 'give them everything' idea is somewhat overdone.

Again and again, in the course of conversation, this topic cropped up. 'We had a talk on the new Homes at the W.R.I.,' said a woman at Craigellachie, 'and we heard that some of the children get up to ten shillings a week pocket money. Oh, I know they're supposed to save off it, and buy toothpaste and stuff, but next day all the women were blazing mad. "We'll all need to send our bairns to Aberlour," they said. "They'll be better off there. *We* canna afford to give them ten shillings a week." '

It went on and on, in various versions. 'It's no use their asking me for money now. They're buying everything new, and I've to make do with second-hand stuff. Surely they could have used what they had, instead of throwing it away.'

'There's collecting boxes in the village, but hardly anybody puts anything in. They feel it's not needed now.'

The new venture is indeed an interesting, if costly, experiment. One hopes that it will be successful, but I feel that perhaps its sponsors should have gaed more warily with their money. They may eradicate some of the snags of orphanage living, but . . . in all honesty, I cannot say that I wish my days at Aberlour had never been. As Wolfie once said at our fireside, discussing and assessing the new plans, and the implied criticism of the old, 'The great thing is, whatever you and other people thought of the place, you came back.'

That, I think, is the crux of the matter. We came back.

With the buildings coming down before our eyes, we couldn't stay away. We went often into the church, which, being separate from the orphanage, was untouched, and we remembered the days when it was full and murmurous with children, and how we had a full quota of dogs with us every Sunday. They all behaved perfectly, until one day a little brown dog from the village looked in at the open door. Suddenly there was a crazed outbreak of snapping and barking, as a solid ball of fighting dogs rolled along the aisle. Three male and two female voices joined sternly in the uproar, and the intruder was led out by the collar. The other dogs settled down angrily, giving little scowls over their haunches as they turned round in their corners, and 'Let us pray,' said Wolfie, imperturbably.

We could see the congregation too, Geordie Sharp the gardener, in his boots and plus-fours, feeding us surreptitious peppermints during the sermon; old Mummie Yates, who, they said, had died in the gatehouse, with her cats waiting hungry by the bed; and Mr. White, the Treasurer, singing lustily. . . .

Mr. White was the man who perfected the double sweet-scented begonia.

There is, at the moment, no such thing as a double sweet-scented begonia, but years ago John Gillam White propagated one and received the R.H.S. silver medal in recognition.

Mr. White was a charming old man in a baggy navy-blue suit, and a way of ambling about with his hands in his sleeves, peering hard through thick glasses before he recognised anybody. He was one of Canon Jupp's original orphans, and by his own efforts he had educated himself and gained an M.A. at Aberdeen University. Since then he had married, and lived with his wife and two daughters in the village, coming up every day to work at the office and run the orphanage finances. He was a quiet man, with a passion for cricket and a reputation for being a bit of a weather prophet. He kept a rain gauge in the gardens, and was always consulted about the prospects for Lossie Day.

But, above all, he loved gardening, and he used the orphanage greenhouses to grow and experiment with all sorts of flowers. At that time the orphanage ran a flourishing line in the sale of daffodil and narcissus bulbs and begonia tubers. Mr. White was an expert in begonias, and his great wish was to propagate a double bloom with a scent.

One day he succeeded. He went rushing along the drive with a flower in his hand, laughing and leaping like a boy, jumping into the air and letting out wild whoops. The boys stared, more worried than amused. Whitey's behaviour was completely out of character. He whirled round a corner, where a boy, Harry Buck, was walking quietly, and thrust the flower under his nose.

'Here! Smell that, boy. What's it like, eh? What does it smell like?'

Startled, Harry recoiled, then sniffed nervously. 'It—it smells nice, sir,' he said.

Mr. White gave another leap into the air. 'Fine, fine! Good boy! You're a *very* good boy!' and he slapped a half-crown into Harry's hand, and dashed off again.

'I honestly thought he'd gone mad,' said Harry, telling me about it. 'I didn't know what I'd done to deserve all that money. Of course, we heard about it afterwards, but we didn't realise. . . .'

The orphanage, however, was quick to cash in on the discovery, and J. G. White's begonias made a great deal of profit on the side. And then the war came. There was hardly any staff to look after the gardens, and those who were left had to concentrate, like everyone else, on digging for victory. The beautiful flower-beds became neglected, the greenhouses were untended; and by this time Mr. White had died, and his secret died with him. He left no notes, and the strain died out. If anyone else wants to try to repeat his accomplishment, they won't be able to begin where he left off. They will have to start from scratch.

We looked at his grave in the snowy churchyard. We read the names on the war memorial, my brother's name among them, and we haunted the drives and broken buildings. The McCorquodale dining hall was having its beautiful parquet floor lifted (oh, the gas light shining on it in long lanes, and the whisper of feet, and the clash of spoons, and the long murmur of prayers!). Now the owls and pigeons flew in at the gaping windows, and it was cold, cold. The dayrooms were deserted, the kitchen ranges rusty. It was almost unbearable, but we couldn't keep away.

We took photographs, the church interior, the hollow walls, and the marvellous view from the front, Ben Aigen humping purple through the birch branches against a snowy sky. But photographs were not enough. We wanted something more tangible to take with us. We coaxed the owner of the buildings to give us one of the ornamentations from the roof. 'You can have it for two pounds,' he said. 'That's wrought iron, you know. It would cost you ten pounds to have it made.'

We met a lot of old friends that week, but, inevitably, there were gaps. Mr. Robinson, the headmaster, had died a few years ago, Mrs. Wolfe and Hilary had been killed recently in a car crash, and Miss McKee and her sister were both dead. Identical as ever, they ended their days bent double with arthritis, but indomitable and mentally erect to the last. And Mr. Leslie himself had died suddenly, after a very short term of office, without being able to see the fruits of his labours.

One grey morning we spent an hour in the graveyard with the caretaker's assistant, Bill Garden, who had married my brother's widow. Here there were other friends we had missed: the Misses Davidson, their small headstone already crumbling; Miss Thirde, whose little shop we so often visited, and so many other worthies of the village. And yet it was comforting to pass by and know that they were there. It was as if the past had not completely gone.

On our last day we paid a final visit to the orphanage, and this time, clambering about inside the building, I realised that I was at last standing in the middle of the green courtyard where the sundial or birdbath had been. Yes, this was it! Here was the stone pedestal, and here the encircling walls and windows; but . . . where was the dining hall? Where had it been? Once again, I was disorientated, and now I would never know.

One last journey round, looking at it long and solemnly, lest we should forget. One more visit to the church. After that it was a whirl of handshakes and good-byes and haste-ye-backs. The baker gave us a parcel of cake and shortbread 'for a wee fly cuppie', and we reluctantly set off for the first leg of our journey home.

The boys met us at Queen Street, their eyebrows raised at our 'wee souvenir', the wrought-iron curlicue which was about the size and weight of a tombstone. Suddenly we realised how much we had missed them. There was a hot supper ready for us when we arrived, daffodils on the table, and greetings cards on the sideboard. We were as glad to be home as we were to visit that other home of so many years ago. Maybe we have had the best of both worlds.